YOUR HANDWRITING AND WHAT IT MEANS

FORMERLY TITLED: THE PSYCHOLOGY OF HANDWRITING

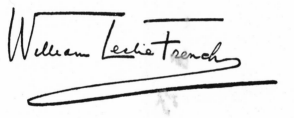

D1127154

npc

NEWCASTLE PUBLISHING COMPANY, INC.
P.O. Box 7589   Van Nuys, Calif. 91409

1976

Dedicated to

WILLIAM GLENNEY FRENCH
and
ELIZA FALCONIE McGEORGE

AN OPINION

By

Harrington Emerson

THE biggest things in the universe are the stars, also the smallest, since even the most powerful telescope opens up new worlds.

The brain was able to evolve eyes and interpret the vibrations of ether so as to reveal to us the infinitely great. The infinitely little gives me great respect for that modified piece of skin called the brain, skin so tough that it can touch glowing coals without injury, so sensitive that thought will make it quiver.

The human brain is capable of taking in through sight the infinitely great and the infinitely little and interpreting it. There are thousands of children, who if placed in the uttermost confines of our solar system would recognize the same constellations; the few, a dozen stars out of the hundreds of millions. What a train of thought the word "Mother" brings up out of the 600,000 words of the English language! How wonderful are the perceptions of the gambler who knows the cards after he has once handled them so that in European gambling clubs, only new packs are used.

While I am personally deficient in keen observation, would never make a good gambler or be able to see the moons of Jupiter with the naked eye, or even to recognize my own brother if I met him unexpectedly in a strange city, I, nevertheless, know that there are men who have powers of observation, trained by practice, and synthetized by good judgment, and these men I employ as specialists when I need their knowledge.

In Germany, as well as other European Countries, a vast literature has grown up, on the subject of Graphology,—The Science of interpreting handwriting. Permanent characteristics, talents, the emotions, and incipient insanity are all revealed in the writing of individuals.

There are men who have the natural ability to interpret handwriting and who have supplemented this ability by much experience and study.

William Leslie French is one whose gifts I have tested.

On various occasions I submitted to Mr. French samples of handwriting, not of strangers, but of people I know very well. From these samples he was able to give advice that I recognized as good. I felt that it would be safe to be helped by him as to people I did not know.

The following are samples of Mr. French's skill:

I submitted a social letter. Mr. French instantly said, "The writer has literary ability and would write well on such a scientific subject as metallurgy." The next mail brought me from the writer two pamphlets on the technicalities of cast iron. Mr. French made many other observations as to this specimen, some of them inspiring confidence, others putting me on my guard.

Another specimen! Mr. French stated at once, "The writer is recklessly extravagant, absolutely unfitted for any commercial career, but also a person of big conceptions." Here again I found both warning and encouragement.

In a third case he said, "It would be advisable never to employ this person for detailed work. Always in a hurry, never stops, plunges straight ahead! But a remarkable critical faculty is indicated."

Here again were warnings and encouragements.

In each of these three cases I knew the writer well.

In a fourth instance, a man came to me with a large business project.

An Opinion

Mr. French seeing a letter from him, replied, "This man is ugly when angry, irritable, not wholly reliable, showing the external pensigns of mental breakdown or even paresis. Do not associate with him in business as he is obstinate, determined, and not amenable to reason. He has energy, force, perseverance; would make a good salesman, and a fair executive, being preëminent in technical work."

With these warnings and admonitions how much better I am fitted to negotiate with this man! If I want him for a technical investigation—Yes—, for a salesman—Perhaps—, for a business associate—No—!

I have weighed Mr. French's ability and often consult him, and having heard what he sees, I decide for myself and often wish later that I had given more weight to his statements.

Every man is interested in himself, as to what he is best fitted for, as to special faults and special qualities. He ought to be interested as to incipient and impending weaknesses. Every man can therefore test on himself Mr. French's ability.

If he finds him reliable and skilled, as I have found him, he can, if he is wise, consult him as to the characteristics of other people.

Mr. French was originally recommended to me by the editor of one of our leading scientific journals and he has written on his subject for a number of the prominent periodicals.

I cordially recommend him as a man able to see much where I can only see a little; but his methods I can understand, . . . minute observation, classification, analysis, synthesis, generalizations.

It is coming more and more to be realized that no man can escape from himself or even hide himself from others. Both in Germany and in this country Institutes exist for the express purpose of analyzing men and women.

There are two problems: to find the right man for a position, to find the right position for a man.

How often is either problem solved?

How many men do you know who are absolutely fit for their positions?

An Opinion

Caruso, Charlie Chaplin, Jack Dempsey, Foch, Kreisler, Lloyd George, Herbert Hoover, Cardinal Mercier! What are their rewards? What would a man have been worth who could have stopped the world war?

Even if we count down the great stars we can avoid the misfits and that is perhaps the greater half of the battle.

PREFACE

In preparing this series of articles and other material which is cognate to the Psychological aspects of handwriting, I have arranged the contents so that it is adapted to the general reader and student. The principles of this science are embodied in the numerous observations and conclusions that I have made plain without unnecessary comments.

Each chapter contains some of the underlying principles of handwriting psychology as applied to some phase of human endeavor, commercial advancement, or protection and such information as is relative to characteristic traits, aptitudes and talents which are revealed. In my own experience I find that the text is best accompanied with the illustrations numbered in series, adapted to each specific topic as discussed. In closing, my belief is that this science if properly employed is valuable in offering an accurate solution for every human problem.

W. L. F.

CONTENTS

xiv   Contents

The Psychology of Handwriting

CHAPTER I

INTRODUCTION

"The Moving Finger writes; and, having writ,
Moves on: nor all your Piety nor Wit
Shall lure it back to cancel half a Line,
Nor all your Tears wash out a Word of it."

ON account of the close relationship existing between an individual and his writing, the signs set down in one form or another may symbolize his entire personality. Writing becomes even to the ordinary observer, the index of strength of character, will power, judgment, and passion—and reveals fully the class of people whom one would choose for associates.

Now the mind employs the brain as the medium through which it issues its commands. Here is life in the brain or mind. It produces certain movements and gestures through the nerves and muscles. This produces ideas, mental processes which are possibly due to chemical changes, sentiments and emotions, all of which are translated into written actions. We classify these handwriting symbols in the same fashion as a botanist who classifies plants according to climate, environment, or habits. Likewise, the chemist tests the elements with which he experiments, making minute analyses and works to secure accurate results. So the handwriting Psychologist studies and arranges his specimens and interprets the significance attached to a wide and varied

3

number of hand-movements. Through observation, he judges each small group of inscribed signs which are more or less energetic, intense, or calm. He recognizes that the writer controls his pen or pencil, if he writes naturally. But his mind impels him to write. The sign-gestures are reflections of invisible mental operations, processes. The cerebral movements are transmitted to and from the nerve centers. The sign-values are permanent, but also occasionally transitory and variable.

All that is necessary to consider is that the impulses which are transmitted from the brain to the fingers differ, in degree, with each person, setting him apart from his fellows; and by comparing the strength or weakness of strokes with the particular formations which appear, it is possible to reach an accurate conclusion.

So people are divided into groups in accordance with their like-nesses or dissimilarities of pen formations. The English writer, Disraeli says, "Handwriting bears an analogy to the character of the writer, as all voluntary actions are characteristic."

It is a common occurrence with us all to recognize the script of our friends and acquaintances. We do it at sight, automatically, in the same way that we know the tones of voice.

The science of reading character from handwriting is a simple one, if the principles laid down are followed. At the outset, it is self-evident to everyone that bodily weakness affects the steadiness of the hand. In wielding the pen, the person's force and stamina being lowered, the features of the writing become altered, reflecting such debility. No malady to which we are heirs but stretches its tentacles along the nerves, getting the muscles in their firm grasp, and this retards freedom of movement. For this reason a change is made in an individual's usual style.

Everywhere, children by their simple, half-formed writing, show that their bodies have not become hardened or their characters fully developed. From No. 1, one can tell at a glance that this writing reflects a character and mentality in the process of growth. The uncertain slant and the halting, stilted manner of making the words

and crossing the t, betray this. In like manner, the advance of old age
leaves traces in wavering and tremulous lines, frequently the last words

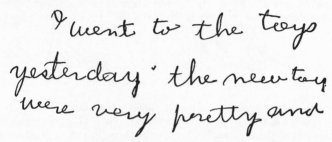

No. 1. A child shows his unformed character by his unformed writing

inclining downward to the right. No. 2 is a fair example—a woman
past eighty.

It requires no necromancy to determine, by a single glance, which
of the two specimens, Nos. 3 and 4, shows the greater amount of force,

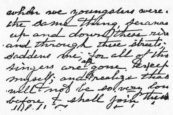

No. 2. Aged woman

strength, and character. These were written by two lads, fifteen years
of age, schoolmates. Both appear, as you see them, to be healthy
youngsters, interested in athletics, bright and intelligent; but their
handwriting reveals something entirely different and more important.

The script of No. 3—light, weak, the strokes penned without care—betrays a lack of purpose and will. The *t*-crossing is uncertain, as if he were not sure of himself. In the formation of his words and letters little determination or power is revealed. He moves over the page as

No. 3.   Betrays a lack of purpose and will

though it were a great mental effort. This utter weakness of pen-force is a positive sign of his being unable to say "No." It is the key-note of his composition. Desire to do may be there, but the will to act is variable.

In strong contrast is the penmanship of No. 4. His pen hits the paper as if he knew what he wanted—always, and was going to get it. He crosses his t's with a heavy, bold stroke; and, combined with the uniform pressure throughout, it signifies that will-power and physical

No. 4.   Shows obstinacy, grit, ambition

endurance are his best endowments. Note the obstinacy and grit in the down stroke of the *y's* below the line, ending hammer-like. They proclaim that he will never be the under dog, that ambition holds him in its grip. He writes up-hill the unfailing mark of a desire to excel. No. 3 uses the same slant, showing that he, too, is ambitious; but it is a flabby ambition. If he does not pull himself together, he will amble along through life, ever requiring a prod to make him achieve anything worth while.

No. 5 shows a person who is in perfect physical and mental health. The steady even pressure and extension of the long letters *g* and *y* below the lines, indicate a robust constitution. There is not a nervous

No. 5.   A man of seventy, but holding his mental and physical health to such a degree that his vigor shows

or erratic dash anywhere.   This writer—a man close to seventy—has never had an illness in his life.   Also, energy, force, ambition, all appear in his rapid style, slightly upward, and in his *t* bar.   This is strong and firm, showing a strong will.

To show the various effects that fatigue and the use of liquor produce in handwriting the following group is wonderfully illuminating. These seven men were congregated in a café one morning at two o'clock. The first shows high tension in the jerky nervous manner of forming his words, the dotting of the *i's*, and the question mark.   In reality, he was under mental stress and worried.   He was drinking to keep himself awake.   A person of his vivid imagination—shown by the high loops of his *h's*—should never drink.   When normal, his writing is vertical and very even.   His beverage was beer, of which he was drinking to excess.   By profession he is a literary man of which his script is a very good example.   The second is that of a strong, full-blooded Irishman, as is seen in the heavy pressure.   But, although he pounds the page as if he were shouting at the same time, shown by his *t*-crossings and quick flowing style, still the *th* is smudged and his physical force is gradually weakening.   Note the tobogganing of "tonight." He also was absorbing beer in copious volumes.

The third typifies energy misdirected, for the force, together with the slant, shows that affection is translated into animal self-indulgence. This individual had been out late, with little or no sleep for a day or two. There is very little sign of nervousness, for he was too young to have been affected by the use of liquor to any extent.

The fourth, by the firm, steady, even pressure, indicates that he is in good condition every way; no flagging of words or lines. He is temperate at present.

But what a contrast in the fifth!

Naturally, he has a clear intellect, as is shown by the upright script, small letters low in height, and one or two of the words well made. That he is a good raconteur appears in the *a's* and *o's* being open at the top. But his holograph goes all to pieces, exhibiting a lack of continuity, caused by the utter failure of his brain to co-ordinate aright. "Moon" and "night" reflect the gradual paralysis creeping over his faculties, intensified by a complete letting down of his mental powers. The words drop lower and lower as if he were about to fall prone and utterly exhausted. And such was the case, though it might be only temporary. He had been drinking every kind of beverage, whiskey predominating.

The sixth and seventh were written by two healthy, virile young men—street car conductors, who had come in from a run of from fifteen to eighteen hours. Each took only a glass of beer and a sandwich. Their penmanship shows physical strength, found in the down strokes, but also shows that they were dead tired. Their formations run down hill, even though the words hit the page upward.

The above instances show beyond cavil that moral degeneration will manifest itself in a weakening of the symbols of expression and, on the other hand, as one's character and nature become stronger, so the symbols likewise become more vital and powerful.

In view of these illustrations, it is necessary to show that the hand movements of human beings are to be considered according to their importance.

No. 6
First

What is the matter the moon tonight?

No. 7
Second

What is the matter with the moon tonight?

No. 8
Third

What is the matter with the moon to-night?

No. 9
Fourth

What is the matter with the moon to-night?

No. 10
Fifth

What with modern with y moon to night?

No. 11
Sixth

No. 12
Seventh

What is the matter with the moon tonight
What is the matter with the moon to night

SEVEN AT TWO IN THE MORNING

Numbers one to three and number five were drunk or nearly. The last two were dead tired
Each one of them shows his condition plainly

No. 1. Energy and will-power, force and determination;—The activity is wavering, nerveless, violent, or emphasized.

No. 2. Speed and vitality:—Animated or slow, abrupt, accelerated or very slow.

No. 3. The direction:—Ascending, or descending.

No. 4. The form:—Angular or coarse (grossly vulgar) rounded or delicate in shape.

No. 5. The frequency of the signs:—The number, those accentuated, or with occasional marked strength. When a sign so displayed but regularly, then an established habit is shown.

No. 6. Letters:—These are carefully joined or disconnected.

No. 7. The extensions:—Ample or short.

By making an examination of these movements and combine such as are evident, we arrive at standards of handwritings which are typical. They are found in all classes of society. There are numerous varieties, but these have to be treated individually. We have to seek special signs which will modify the peculiarities or accentuate them. For example, a specimen may exhibit some curious forms which will have to be examined for erotic, temperamental conditions or intensity of emotion. Then the strokes will present an unusual formation. The types are as follows:

No. 1. The cool logical thinker.
" 2. The calm, ambitious, determined, writer.
" 3. The phlegmatic or even lazy individual.
" 4. The loose imaginative person whose ideas are hazy.
" 5. The violent, vulgar, or an individual with little control over the passions and the desires and appetites.
" 6. The nervous form.
" 7. The hysterical.

Many people express their doubt about the utility of this science. They cannot see how character can be analyzed or talents shown on account of the fact that there are so many different signs, all varying. Now the following diagram explains to the uninitiate as well as others how the process works out in making a delineation. The specimens attached were taken from a letter written by one individual.

The inner circle represents Mind. The arrow shows the changes which modify a person's *tout ensemble*, as it passes from one point to the others.

Introduction

(1) The vertical style with uniform pressure gives the man mental poise, force, and some obstinacy, as the blunt ending of some strokes denotes.

(2) The small low letters reveal his power of concentration.

(3) The upward slant signifies ambition and some enthusiasm.

(4) The wide spacing between his words and letters is the sign of generosity.

(5) This trait appears again with very remarkable *t* bars. They are firm but extend too far to the left, showing will power rather strong at times, but also a tendency to procrastination.

(6) The long capital *Y* is the mark of great egotism and conceit.

(7) The long extended rounded stroke of the *y's* gives him great power of endurance. The last letter with its peculiar curve would show him to be erratic and even eccentric.

(8) This endows him with rapidity of thought and action.

(9) This artistically formed capital *D* gives an inordinate love of approbation, shown by its height, but also a devotion to art in all of its forms. The down and cross shading denotes that his five senses are on the alert every minute.

(10 and 11) The angle of his writing changes, betokening vacillation, and even moodiness; depression also appears in the downward flow of the word formation, "worried."

(12) The sharpening of some of the small letters at the top are the mark of a keen critical faculty; but the wavy base line and this pointed style shows that he would falsify deliberately.

(13) Here the last-mentioned qualities appear, together with small letters of uneven height—inconsistency.

(14) The rounded swing of the words at the bottom reveal a marked love of music, both melody and harmony. In fact, this is shown, to a greater or less degree, all through.

(15) Here are found extreme forms which likewise are seen elsewhere. The "M" signifies that he is original in his high rigid hand movement. Muscles contracted. No. 16, Again, his "recovered" is similar to his style in "yesterday."

To sum up his characteristics, he has a keen intelligence, more or less mentally careless at times, irascible, often erratic, impulsive and generous. Selfish only when his pleasures are interferred with, belonging to the group termed temperamental. Artistic, musical, he has a gift for literary production, with a big imagination. He loops his long letters above the line. He would borrow freely and is extravagant, pleasure-loving and inclined to self-indulgence. His inclinations are such as would cause him to procrastinate, and then suddenly apply himself to any work in which he is interested. But he will never be efficient, as his will-power and self-control are variable.

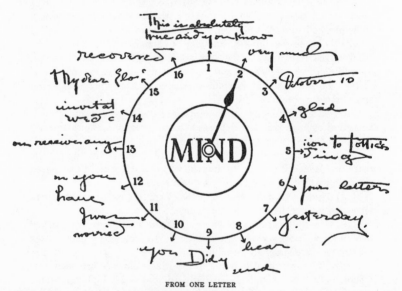

FROM ONE LETTER

No. 13.   The diagram explains to the uninitiate, as well as to others, how the process works out in making a delineation

Introduction

To judge a specimen of handwriting, it is necessary that it should be written naturally, normally, in ink, with at least twenty to thirty words with the signature or at least the initials. The ideas in the writing should be inscribed without apparent forethought.

The signature is the summing up of the characteristics which are found in the body of the script.

Now many series of experiments have been verified for years and the conclusions are here submitted in the subsequent material, presented in numerous and varied topics in their consecutive order.

A wide survey of human movements in their manifestations and interpretations are plainly exhibited. The subject matter is arranged so that it is comprehensive and readily understood. With each topic there are special groups of individuals whose tendencies, characteristics, aptitudes, mental and physical phenomena, are analyzed, supplementing the significance of the text. The casual reader or student will appreciate that script signifies one phase of life which is positive, definite, and accurate.

CHAPTER II

INDEX TO YOUR PHYSICAL AND MENTAL STATE

"William Leslie French, is widely known as an authority on the psychology of handwriting. He has lectured for years on this subject and has written many magazine articles on various phases of it. His experiments in every field include examinations of specimens written by insane persons, criminals, drug addicts and others afflicted with various physical disabilities.

"An interesting angle of Mr. French's work has been in the business field where his analyses of applications for positions have decided the employment or non-employment of many responsible executives."

THERE is one standard by which people, both men and women are judged in every condition and walk of life. That is, "by your actions and character you win or lose." And this standard is formed consciously or unconsciously by the numerous impressions which each one receives from associates, friends, and strangers also. We judge an individual from his gait, his expression, his manner of speech, but these frequently are misleading.

A person whose usual disposition is energetic, buoyant, lively, and optimistic naturally employs upward and free gestures. Any one who has a leaning toward depression, either temporary or permanent, will exhibit a limp, weak and exhausted fashion of gesticulating. His or her arms and hands are devitalized! And if you observe from the standpoint of handwriting only you will note that the script gestures of each will correspond—the jovial, cheerful optimist using a rapid flowing upward trend to the right, the pessimist permitting his inky impressions to decline, line upon line, word after word, downward in the same direction.

That handwriting is regarded as an index to certain mental conditions is well known. If you have ever consulted a nerve specialist one of the first questions which he will ask is, "Have you paid any attention to the way you write? Do you notice that your hand does not act with freedom or is uncertain in its action? If so, it will help me to arrive at a better diagnosis of your case." His years of experience tell him that any variation in script forms may have some special significance, that a nervous quiver or vagary has a story to relate concerning the nerves and their relation to an individual's mental state and thus he is able to treat his case with greater exactness. A little scrap of paper, but how significant!

ALIENISTS' TEST

Also, it is a common thing for an alienist to demand a specimen of handwriting in order to help him determine whether his patient has delusions, is insane, or is carried away by certain emotions or any abnormality. And there is a reason for this. It has been proved many times that there is a distinct relation between the nerves of the brain and those of the hand, so that a man's writing reflects his mental temperature.

In like fashion you, too, when feeling out of sorts or lacking in your accustomed energy or force, can easily see slight changes appearing in your script which are not quite up to normal. Then it is that you should begin to look after your personal welfare, both physical and mental. It is your guide that points what should be your road to travel.

Now it is interesting to note that when people are in good health of both body and mind that irrespective of their style they will employ uniform pressure throughout, make their connecting strokes of words and letters with one movement of the pen and extend their long letters, such as g, j and p, well below the base line, which at the same time may be either looped or straight down. You will observe at once the balanced arrangement of words, while the spacings between lines will be uniform. The capital letters are usually in proportion to the lower case and in most instances the "t" bars will be formed with decision and force. No hesitancy!

SHOWS FIRM WILL

No. 1 is an excellent illustration of a man who has great physical and intellectual vitality, strong recuperative powers, accompanied by a firm will. He would ever be poised for action and show courage. Then

No. 1

compare this specimen with that penned by some individuals whom you know well and you would find that they are not easily disturbed, do not go up in the air at trifles and their actions could be relied upon. You would understand why they are considered solid and vital in their social and commercial relationships. Having clean, wholesome bodies their pen gestures reflect sound intellects.

In this connection it follows that the writer possesses alertness, thinks quickly, or at least clearly, and will carry out his ideas with ease.

In the case of No. 2, a woman, although her style is quite dissimilar her "t" crossings unlike and her word formations her own, still she shows the same healthful appearance. Her down pressure is decided, firm and well distributed and any one would say at first glance that she is the type who knows her own mind.

In vivid contrast with No. 3 you will at once conclude that this woman writer's hand is not affected to any extent when handling her pen. But she gives clear evidence that her muscles and nerves are under perfect control. Her strokes are positive, her mental action likewise.

But what an erratic, distorted picture is shown by No. 3! He crawls across the page as if guided and impelled by some strange uncontrolled force which makes radical changes in the formations of nearly every word. This man's nerves are on the jump, a-jangle,

No. 2

quivering and in his desire and worry to write correctly his pen leaps here and there as though uncertain of the next movement. Note how

No. 3

his lines slant downward to the right, revealing exhaustion and a depressed condition of mind. His strokes are feeble, although at the beginning of a new line there is an upward direction, indicating that by nature he was very forceful, energetic and determined—his ink flows easily and heavily, but he has not the stamina to continue. This writer is a nervous wreck. You can see readily that he is utterly lacking in self-control and balance. If he had known that his writing would reflect his physical condition at the start he could have taken the ordinary precautions, watched his pen movements and, regulating his habits, he might now find himself where he could control these tremors and be a well man. There are many other illustrations where these signs are not so pronounced, but when they appear it is common sense to observe their significance.

SIGNIFIES INTENSE IMAGINATION

In numerous types of handwriting the manner of throwing the looped t's, l's and other long letters to excess above the line become the most striking feature, one which catches the eye immediately. Whenever this formation appears it symbolizes the existence of a startling, vivid, intense imagination, which gives the writer a mental trend which will overbalance other qualities and produce the effect of high nervous tension and a lack of poise.

No. 4

Too great emotion! No. 4 especially illustrates that her imaginative faculty is running rampant, so dominating this writer, so swaying her every thought that her actions are marked by excitement, vacillation, moodiness and even her speech. At the start she flies upward with large, flamboyant flourishes as if to say, "I have a great idea for a story and I know that I can sell it anywhere. I am going right home and write." But she never does!

The angle of her words changes, her ideas change also. Her arm and hand weaken, relax, while her words slant downward in a melancholy fashion with not enough buoyancy actually to finish her final strokes aright. You will observe that naturally she has much physical vitality, as is shown by the long looped extensions of long letters below the line. Both men and women who exhibit these signs are endowed with much vivacity, spring and elasticity.

SHOULD EXERCISE

Such individuals should take regular and persistent exercise in the open so that they can hold in check their tendencies to intensity of thought and emotion. The excessive use of coffee, tea or stimulants will increase their natural propensities and sooner or later they will go to pieces. Curiously enough where these exaggerated forms are found then the desire and unnatural craving exist—something to take the place of the energy lost by emotion. Still, the very existence of the partially high looping of the l's and other long letters above the line is advantageous, for it indicates that the writer is gifted with big vision, is far sighted and, other traits being evenly developed, will be successful. These looped forms appear in the handwriting of many able and efficient people in all walks of life.

No. 5 reveals the hallmarks pointing to keen vision and shrewd intelligence, reënforced by steady, even pressure and excellent connections. The looped signs referred to, when examined with reference to mental and physical poise as here shown, indicate that such writers are sure to be responsible in all of their actions. Naturally there are many varieties as to type, but like the man with a wooden leg, easily recognized—the pen-gait tells!

very much that's cannot go beyond the limit subscribed,

No. 5

With No. 6 there is evidence of remarkable strength and abundant vitality. This writer has spent the larger portion of his life in wide wind-blown spaces, having arrived at the age of fourscore and ten, being still hale and hearty. He has never had a severe illness in his life, so he says, and his direct, straightforward script is indicative of

With kind regards,

James Deniston

No. 6

his rugged honesty of statement, apart from anything else. His is the domination over muscle, nerve and mind, for every stroke is powerful with ink and the firm even flow, vigorous assurance in every word, is significant of courage, will power, determination and restless activity. Do you note any weak spot, any sudden or erratic splashes? You do not!

PERFECT PHYSICAL POISE

There is almost perfect physical poise and consequently he has the intellect to match it. His specific achievements in his part of this country are on record and they reflect the soul of the man. Having had the opportunity of examining many specimens of lounge lizards, night hawks, both male and female, I would say that if they began to care for their bodies in the manner such as this writer, they will live to enjoy life to the full when they get older, and be of some use to society at large. Their pen-formations do not lie!

Naturally there are many cases where healthy physiques are accompanied by weak mentalities, and the reverse. However, when this happens, you will find here and there through the writing certain peculiar or rare signs which to the trained expert signify those tendencies, which would not be apparent to others. Frequently this is shown when an individual has had a severe illness, which deprives him of his ability to think and act rationally. In some portion of his script alterations will appear, which may have been caused by delirium or fever-hallucinations. And these changes are self-evident to the discerning eye.

The examples shown in Nos. 7 and 8 were written by a man who had had a severe nervous illness and had partly recovered. At first

No. 7

glance they appear to be quite dissimilar. But there is a general likeness displayed in the fleet swing, well-made connections, small letters sharpened at the top, with the fashion of word formation as in "you," which is one point of identification. The first is plainly written by one who has pretty good control over his hand—evidenced by the balance and steady movement throughout.   That which was inscribed

No. 8

later on is abnormai, irregular, revealing hurried extended "t" dashes and a decided weakening of the lines at the end as if his fingers and hand had utterly relaxed, strengthless or nearly so.

His unaccustomed dashes indicate high tension and nervous excitability, while the break between some of his word-forms shows that the writer held his breath for a moment before he continued his writing. In addition this very uncertainty in using his fist would have a reaction upon his mind and thus effect a further transformation.   Still the construction of words and letters is practically alike in form.   They remain constant in the same way as the bony structure of the hand remains, reflecting the writer's original endowment which holds steadily through good health and ill.   When a person recovers his strength his writing also takes on a like color and assumes the original structure.

Now as a short illness of severity will depress the usual swing and slope for a brief time, and temporary moods produce alterations in the script, so a person under great stress of emotion or trouble will exhibit some marked changes, if only for the time being.   No. 9 was dashed off by a person who had just heard of the death of a relative.   Under normal conditions this writing runs across the page with an even base line, but here there is a noticeable weighing down of the line at the end. A melancholy state of mind.

Once in a while one is able to secure a specimen of some medical man who is subject to extreme nervous attacks; and No. 10 was written

by an eminent surgeon just after he had finished a big operation which
tasked his nerve and left him in a tense condition. You will note that

No. 9

his connections are clearly made, and that he uses a uniform pressure
with minutely formed characters—the sign of great power of application. If you met this individual you would be struck by his robust
physique and good color. But his script as herein shown is as tremulous as if he had the palsy and filled with other peculiarities.

No. 10

When he is absent from his work he writes in the same general
manner, but the variations are not evident to even the casual eye. It
is true that after he has completed a skilful operation he immediately
goes away for an extended vacation until he has recuperated. He gave
this for comparative purposes.

As we are in the experimental stage of prohibition, it is interesting
to see to what extent the abuse produces certain and almost fundamental
alterations in their pen-prints. Some under the influence of liquor, if
very drunk, will scrawl in every direction. Others under like stimulation will write with greater firmness, but under a powerful glass, there
will appear peculiar quivers which to the naked eye would not be

displayed. The fact is that narcotics and stimulants all have their own external signs which are easily recognized if one takes the trouble to look for them.

An individual with whom I am acquainted writes to me quite frequently, and with his permission I submit two specimens of his script, one written before he went off on a debauch, the other indited just after he had partly recovered. He is the type who swears intelligently whenever he gets under the influence, and then goes to his country home, where he exercises in the open until recovery. Burning the candle at both ends and in the middle, it seems to me!

No 11 was written in his usual clear clean cut fashion, each word well made and a complete absence of any irregularities. When he

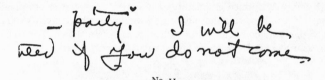

No. 11

writes in this way he exhibits keen intelligence, is forceful and logical and shows every evidence of being in control of his actions and physically strong. It is easy to see that when he penned No. 12 he was upset

No. 12

and disturbed. His tracks wander hither and thither, he jerks his pen with a quiver and fires his "t" bars and "i" dottings as if he were under some great excitement of delirium.

His natural script is rounded, indicating a decent disposition, but here he sharpens it as if his intellect was pointed with irritation, a mass of sensitive angles, each one on the jump, It looks drunk. It was, and he also. Examine this under a powerful lens and you would see that the edges of some of the down strokes are jagged with fine teeth. The word appearing in each exhibit is alike in form. No variation, indicating that his brain still functions in part normally even though blunted in its usual action. It is the connecting link between his two selves, reflecting a dual personality.

"DRUNKS" ARE SUSPICIOUS

One of the hardest things to accomplish is to get people who are swayed by drink to give you a specimen, due to that fact that their very intoxication makes them more or less suspicious. When No. 13 put his

No. 13

pen to paper he was fighting off the effect of the fumes in his knees and brain. It is clear that his writing is quite legible, even though the man had consumed enough mixed drinks to overcome a regular habitué. His writing is fairly even and he shows good pressure, although he exhibits unnecessary scrawls in occasional letters, his pen slipping from a wabbly hand. In this instance the writer still has some control over his mind.

With his companion number (13a) there appears a like pen movement and the signs are a trifle more in evidence. His nib zigzags wofully, as is shown in "fight." I might say that neither of these two is so far gone in the use of stimulants that the "liquor, whiskey or gin

quiver" could be found. They only drink occasionaliy. It is valuable
to realize that one of these men has apparently a good reason for wish-

No. 13a

ing to forget a recent experience. "I was traveling down South
recently," he said, "and an epidemic broke loose on board ship. The
only remedy which prevented those who were still well was hard liquor
and plenty of it. Every one who could was ossified, we lost every day
ten to fifteen. Drink? you bet, or take drugs. For I won't give myself
a chance to get those bugs, even if I am drunk every day." Of course,
he was overwrought, but a cause lay behind his state of intoxication.

Now you would hardly think that coffee and tea have their drunkards, men and women who show peculiar pointed signs in the formation

No. 14

of individual letters or in exaggerated capitals when they have drunk
too much. But it is so. No. 14, a woman, always had her coffee pot
boiling on the stove. She drinks from seven to eight cups in an afternoon, and then some more. Is it any wonder that her script trembles?

If you will look closely you will see that the general force of the writing is there, but modified by the tremble.

Tea drunkards also show some slight variations, but these are not evident to the ordinary eye. The main indications are found where the writing suddenly becomes rather jagged in spots, in the same way as people who have tendencies to heart affections frequently make a break in the lower part of the down strokes of y's and g's. See No. 15.

No. 15

In such cases it really requires an expert psychologist to determine positively, as these special quivers are sometimes alike in form. Those appearing in the script of the aged will often mislead one, for they appear to be similar at first glance, and even the second and the third.

The absintheur also has an interesting exhibit, usually accompanying his regular forms with a shake of his own, flamboyant flourishes and other sprawls—wild extending strokes of the finals of words. No. 16 is one very fair example, written for the writer by a woman who started in when abroad and has kept up the habit, "Just to plague those dry humorists who have got irreligion." And despite the law, she still has a regular "still" on, apparent to none except one who can read the signs in her pen forms.

It may be asked if the drug addict shows an original quiver or shake. He does, but there are several varieties, which run each other a close

second as far as appearance goes. However, No. 17 will give the reader
an idea of what happens when a person has become addicted to mor-

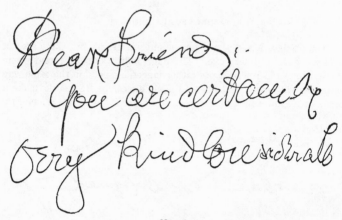

No. 16

phine. Here you see a well-known athlete. His script moves ahead
slowly but firmly, showing the long extensions below the lines—his
natural physical strength and love of sports. Vision this man trying

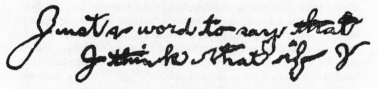

No. 17

to write, his hand working on almost blindly so that his style is stilted.
As you follow his lines and words you note that a slight creep develops
on the side of various letters, and a thickening also appears in parts of

individual letters. His twin shows quite a different exhibit. No. 18.
Did you ever see such an entanglement of lines, and such a smudging

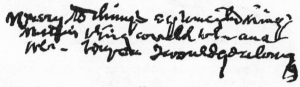

No. 18

of words and letters? This man's script denotes that his brain is working through a fog of confusion.

In presenting these particular observations I wish to show that a
knowledge of this subject is especially valuable because it really covers
every form of human endeavor and becomes a safeguard against disease,
vice and crime, not to speak of its utility in placing individuals in their
proper place in society and the commercial world.

Naturally, when you deal with a great variety of human beings,
where there are many varieties and numerous types, it is possible to
give only such specimens which will present obvious signs so that the
reader will not be confused.

Where the signs referred to above are not developed too greatly,
why there is always time to get control before the tendencies attain
complete mastery. Experience has taught me that when you find you
are using some hesitancy in writing, in penning your signature, then is
the moment for you to stop and consider the why and the wherefore,
before it is too late. This does not mean that you are necessarily in
such a condition that you need to consult a specialist, but merely that
your script is one positive indication that you should look after your
health. In this day and generation, this is wise economy and good
efficiency from both the personal standpoint and that of your family.
The little things count. And handwriting is one of these.

In this connection are typical types who show physical endurance,
strong physiques and clear intelligences.

Rear Admiral, U. S. N. (Retired) Commandant, Navy
Yard and Station

No. 19. Signature written with perfect connections, determined
t-bar, with down strokes heavy below the line.

Lieutenant-Colonel, U. S. Marine Corps, Commanding Marines

No. 20. Pressure uniform, forceful, long extensions sweeping
under the line. Result-producing final.

Captain, U. S. Navy, "North Dakota"
Commanding

No. 21. Script heavily inscribed. Hand-motion finely balanced.

No. 22. The shaded careless style of restlessness, is an aviator's
hand.

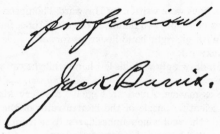

No. 23. Heavy-weight prizefighter.

No. 24. One steady movement with no break in the strength of line. Athlete with world record, 100–200 yds. dash.

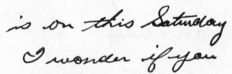

No. 24a. Light-weight boxer.
Here follow a series of handwritings which reflect mental and nervous affections.

No. 25.

The above lines were written by Hayward Thompson to show how his two brains guide his two hands at the same time, but in opposite directions.   With his right hand he writes forward while with his left he writes backward.

But he can draw only with his left hand while he can write forward only with his right.

He is the ex-marine, American Legion "Mystery Man," and the most recent scientific puzzle of the human ruins of the World War. Feb. 2, 1922, is the wall which amnesia, resulting from a terrible head wound, has erected between his present and past.

No. 26.   The nerves of the right hand are affected, so that the writing is modified with quavers.

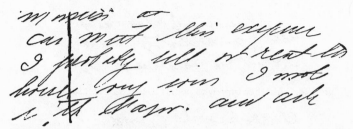

No. 27.   Individual with neurasthenic tendencies.   Intense and emotional.

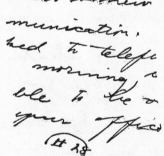

No. 28.   Leaning towards pronounced melancholy and even worse.

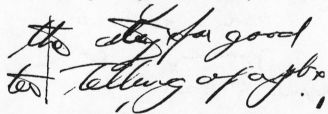

No. 29.   Dementia Præcox.   The mind degenerates slowly with dreams always developing and habits foul.   Note the involutions of several strokes.

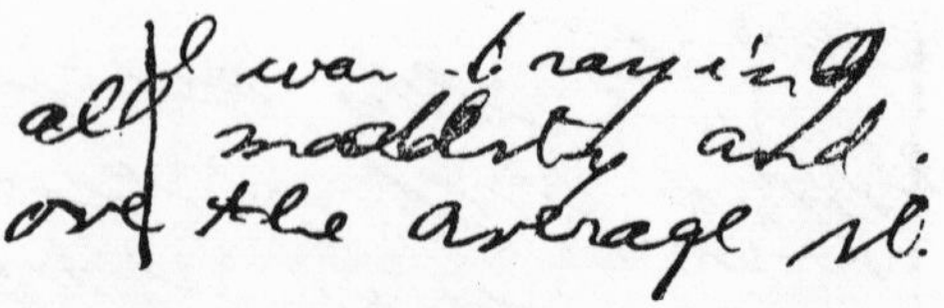

[handwriting specimen]

No. 30.   Another type who points towards Dementia Præcox.

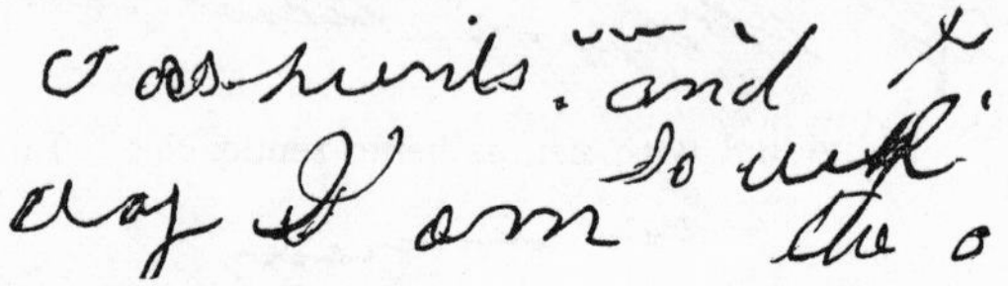

[handwriting specimen]

No. 31.   Locomotor Ataxia.   The movements and ideas are smashed up.

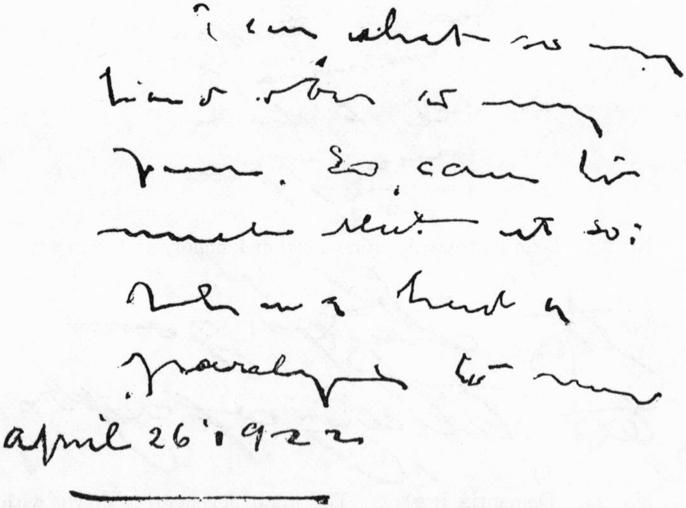

[handwriting specimen]

No. 32.   Written on the second day after the individual had a paralytic stroke.   Observe the degeneration of the strokes and words.

I am feeling a great deal better. But my hand works very slowly.

may 6·22

No. 33.   Note how much stronger the writing is at the later date —10 days.

CHAPTER III

PSYCHOLOGY AND COMMERCIAL LIFE

Employer Tells of Amazing Results Attained by Analyzing Script of His Staff—Typical Examples Cited as Guide in Sizing Up Capabilities.

IN a large room recently a group of business men were seated around a long, flat top table, their faces turned toward the president. As members of the board of directors a grim silence held them. With a slight nod to the vice-president this executive left the chair, and with a sheaf of papers in his hand addressed them.

"In my additional capacity as general manager of this corporation," he said, "this monthly analysis and summary of business, the cost of production and earnings is apparently very bad. Our factories have been running at capacity, and the fault seems to lie with our production manager. In my judgment, 'yes' and 'no.' He has been working like a heavily charged dynamo during the last few months, and his reports have been somewhat irregular. He acts as usual—but——"

His eye swept keenly each intent face. He realized that he was responsible for many policies inaugurated and for the selection of practically the heads of all departments. That his methods had been somewhat radical but progressive he also knew. Thus far his associates had given their full approval. He stopped in rather a dramatic fashion, testing their temper and attitude.

"During the last two years and without your knowledge," he continued, "I have been employing the services of a man who is expert in determining people's fitness for one kind of specialized work or another.   Several of our most skilful managers and salesmen were selected by him as especially adapted for their jobs.   Thus far they have all made good.   He made psychological examinations of their handwriting, having never seen them or received any advance information."

For an instant an audible gasp went forth.

"I had my own handwriting analyzed by him several months before I met him.   Curiosity, if you will.   But when he informed me that salesmanship and executive work with constructive ideas were my specialties, why," he laughed, "I was flattered, but as you know, it is true.   I tested his skill for over six months out of my own pocket, and, gentlemen, seven months back, when the writing of our production manager was submitted for his say so, he gave him the highest recommendation, chosen first out of ten applicants, but he said that his tendency and weakness was to break under great stress of work, and under such conditions his judgment would be likely to become impaired. He would render inaccurate estimates and muddle his reports.   He states further that I could employ him with the assurance that I would secure a star manager, but that details were one of the weak points in his chain.

"It has turned out just as he said.   Here is the typewritten analysis given to me long ago.   Here is another rendered two weeks back on which he says that our man is on the brink of a collapse.   And here is another report made out in longhand which I dug up from our manager's desk, written by him, that shows that his mind was clear then and that our monthly earnings are actually far above what we expected. He broke on the last copy!   Now, this may appear to you to be a bit odd to use this way to convince you, but it pays in our business to safeguard ourselves from every angle.   Else why do we have to pay under the compensation law and use sanitary precautions?   This is just a financial sanitary precaution."

"Well, I'll be d——d!" exclaimed the stubborn and argumentative board member.   "You've got the stranglehold on us as usual, John."

CONFRONTED BY MANY FIRMS

Now this is the situation which confronts many corporations and firms throughout this country. They choose their associates and employees, in numerous instances, either by reputation or recommendation, both of which may be faulty. But if they relied upon the actual evidence as shown by an individual script, given by a competent handwriting psychologist, they would secure an impersonal point of view which would frequently save time, worry and useless expense. For handwriting is a reproduction of a person's traits—his consequent actions and possible dealings. The commercial aspects of script are the result of close comparison and observation—stroke upon stroke.

Take twenty men who hold positions of trust and responsibility and you will find that in many pronounced features there will be marked similarities. Knowing the characteristics of, say three, in their business affiliations and transactions and finding like pen-forms in others, you will discover that these two are replicas in intellectual trend and action. They naturally will fall into the same class.

Now the executive speaking above is a big, far-sighted man, intelligently selfish enough to sacrifice immediate gains for future profits, and to make a wise expenditure to secure a powerful bulwark of human personnel against possible disaster. He is looking for stability and security, which in the management of industrial and commercial affairs are essential. He knows men. Also he is not a profiteer.

No. 1

With No. 1 he introduces himself as a man of force, determination, will-power and acute vision. He pushes his pen with energy and strong hand control. Note the steady, powerful pressure, uniform and exact. His blunted down strokes emphasize his mental alertness, which appears in the perfect connection of his letters. His outlook and broad viewpoint show in the looped "d" and "t" while his judgment can be relied upon, for his spaces between lines and even words are even.

It is evident that this writer knows his own mind. No wabbling! No erratic twists and dashes! Having any large transaction to accomplish every ounce and pound of energy would whirl it to a successful finish. And yet the rounding swing of his rather pointed style, together with the first small letters of words being higher than those following, reveals him to be a man of tact and suavity, but not too suave. His hand is virile with possible fighting activities. Were you acquainted with his signature you would see that his capitals are about the same height and character as that penned by No. 2.

No. 2

SIMILAR IN MANY WAYS

Although these two are far apart in their daily endeavors, their verisimilitude is apparent. Further, both exhibit by their long extended strokes below the lines a superb natural physical strength and endurance which help feed and sustain their mental powers, their resourcefulness. In Mr. Baruch's case the dash made after certain words gives him additional caution.

In exhibit No. 3—a woman—there is displayed an equal decision of character and will to achieve, coupled with innate shrewdness and the capacity for continuous work. Her sharpened script endows her

rather difficult under-taking ; but suppose

No. 3

with a clear understanding mind. That she is able to plan and execute, to see that her ideas are carried out, are denoted by her concentrated style of writing, her even, decided connections and "t" bars. She also has the executive sense.

One fact holds pat with all great executives. The signature is the determining factor, serving as the keystone to the arch of each one's handwriting structure. Of course there are various degrees of this ability. Should the capitals be flamboyant, excessively out of proportion to the small letters or body of the writing, then such a writer would be so dominant and inflated with his own importance that his intrinsic

No. 4

reliability would be impaired. Foreshortened financial vision where his cocksure attitude would preclude his acceptance of suggestions or new policies. Thus disaster would eventually fall upon the corporate interests of which he was the head. And naturally. See No. 4.

The opposite signs obtain as well where the signature is very low and precise.   In some or other administrative capacities connected with our present Government to-day at Washington are a number of these executives who fall into these two ranks.   They cannot help it.   Their signatures are insignificant.   And, alas, they are really insignificant, also.   Should the readers be familiar with any of these writers' script, just observe how easily this statement can be verified.

In this connection it follows that individuals who have marked aptitude for such positions as managers, departmental heads and sales managers possess some qualifications of an executive character.   Still, in addition, the signs which symbolize their special abilities in this respect are clearly shown.

No. 5

The pen traits, which are especially significant in No. 5, are the rapid swing, well-balanced style, positive "t" crossings and even spacing and alignment.   These disclose this person's keen grasp of affairs, his excellent method of reasoning and the will to put every detail into execution without fluster or lack of control.   His comparatively low small letters signify his gift to analyze, systematize and collate, so that all data relative to the various departments under his supervision and guidance would be carefully prepared.   The entire work performed as to earnings and overhead expenses and the progress in all departments he would handle with ease, being always genial toward his subordinates.   His hand is not entirely composed of angles. He has an agreeable disposition and is an approachable man.

HERE IS A VIVID CONTRAST

In vivid relief is No. 6—bad relief, any one can notice the striking difference exhibited. Yet the hallmarks are similar up to a certain point. But this individual through nervous tension and irritabilty, as is shown by the breaks between letters and occasional smudging of

No. 6

strokes and the dashes, exclaims that his usual fair judgment is so modified that he jumps at conclusions, thinks in jerks and quirks, dashing at his duties with an utter lack of poise. His method of directing others would be marked by an endless tendency to discussion. This is indicated by his inflammatory, unevenly shaded strokes, pointed tops, his open "a's" and "o's." Tongueitis is his affliction.

"Curse his fault finding and nagging!" would be heard all along the line, even to the marcelled stenographer and excuse-making office boy. This exhibit is presented so as to make perfectly clear how two men occupying managerial positions and having certain script signs alike may through temperamental conditions be successful or the opposite.

So with No. 7, an equal sex manager, there is a noticeable similarity and dissimilarity to those preceding. Her main features, being an almost forced deliberative style and little quickness of movement with very blunt finals, cause her to feel that she is the leading lady in the establishment. She usually says: "I'm *right*. My figures *are* correct. The sales in my department are *'way* above those of last month." Injured dignity. Her pointed letters are ever ready to impale any reasonable criticism.

You employers know the type.   Well, here is a sample of her writing.
Still, her methodical fashioning of each word, her clearly formed connec-

Every incident of your daily

trade are Educational

No. 7

tions and solid pressure are indices of mental force and enforced supervision.   Reliable.   She writes straight to her ideas, with no uncertain
offshoots.   But you cannot get on without her, for she is a good manager.

THE COLD, CALCULATING TYPE

Dipping into the money honeyed district of our great city, your
attention is called to No. 8, whose brain teems with cold calculation,
facts, figures and finance.   He almost looks as if he were suffering from

Pamphlet over that you left

with me, written by him .

No. 8

jaundice, which he has accumulated from the color of the gold he
handles.   His skill in ferreting out shady depositors, in giving extension
of credits, is found in the angular, penetrating style of his small pointed
letters and cut short and forever finals.   He never mixes the religion of

business with the irreligion of sentiment. Each stroke comes down on a delinquent with a decisive "no" which would be as sharp as his razor. His writing is as immaculatel y accurate as his decisions and his conservative garments.

Sound. finances are credits are essential to business

No. 9

His redeeming feature is that the first small letter of some of his words is higher than those following, as "o" in "over." A cool, dulcet suavity which also is as penetrating as his handwriting eye. His logic is that of a reasoning machine which never slips a cog when it comes to financial transactions. An excellent man in his place.

And the resemblance to this exhibit, pictorially, of efficient credit managers is pronounced, even though in most instances there are the signs of a little more variety in treating humans. Thus No. 9 has the same essential hallmarks. There is less hardness and sharpness in his

f the apostrophe.
And words are en
with the short don

No. 10

down and cross strokes, while his general style is not ossified with granite pen atoms. There is a like keenness, perspicacity, shrewdness, but his easy flow would make him less adamantine in treating those who were behind in their payments,

By contrast the wild, erratic sprawling display of No. 10 removes him far from any real actual capacity for holding down a credit position successfully. Yet this is his job. And only the financial gods can decide—why? You note that his whole script flaunts wide open with a lack of word control, with a tendency to go after collections with pick and shovel. An excellent man to handle Bolshevistic investors in encyclopædias or fictional monstrosities.

Again the expert in statistics indites a hand whose signs are illustrated by No. 11. Observe the close power of application and analytical insight revealed by the carefully, minutely formed, well-balanced

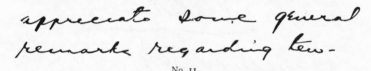

No. 11

words. The sharpened tops of many letters also endow the writer with a fine critical faculty and the ability to discriminate between false and accurate data. His precise punctuation and exact "t-bar" show a high degree of commercial caution.

"No possible shadow of doubt, no possible doubt whatever," but that he would include the uttermost farthing when compiling a statistical report, or any other.

HOW TO TELL GOOD SALESMEN

In selling goods, commodities, ideas, and money or its equivalent there are numerous varieties of script forms displayed, but No. 12 is an excellent illustration of a man who has the ability to sell with bright intelligence and to close contracts. It is evident he has a rapid, well poised swing; a concentrated style and uniform pressure, combined with tightly closed letters and rather high looped extensions above the lines. Here is discovered the quick, energetic talker—convincing, not too persuasive, but able to array his facts with clarity. He would present an argument in favor of his product easily. He rounds his under strokes. His tongue would not run away on a tangent.

No. 12

Imagination is well restrained! His firm fashion of bringing his strokes down straight indicates persistence, firm and sure spoken. So out with his pen at the right moment and your signature to a contract would be signed before you had really grasped his meaning. The general pen-gestures extending upward toward the right resemble the buoyant enthusiasm of a healthy mind, intent and alert to do his work effectively and well. Such writers go abroad with their eyes wide open. They excel in the fields of advertising, space selling, as bonds salesmen or in kindred lines. But they must show most of these signs to be successful if not all.

In this class is No. 13, whose signature if regarded alone, is rampant with self-assurance and big conceptions. He forges ahead with complete disregard of all petty details, for the idea is the main thing with him. Every capital letter proclaims his ability to adapt himself or curve around to novel or unexpected situations. And his pointed style and pronounced connections put arguments upon his lingual flow which would convince a continental banker of his utter inefficient financial acumen.   At times such a vivid redundant style of signature would

No. 13

produce too great enthusiasm.   But the holograph of this writer denotes great and natural talent for promotion—one who can sell and in large quantities.

In view of these two exhibits, would you entrust No. 14 to represent you in the selling field?   I doubt it.   A mere glance will confirm you that the penman ambles along with about as much force and determina-

No. 14

tion as an invertebrate Leghorn pullet which has been reading Mrs. Margaret Sanger on birth control.   His script moves with his gait, one might say, as far as self-confidence is shown.

As the individual who controls the howitzer in commercial organizations is the auditor or accountant, so No. 15 is an example of one whose mental traits enable him to devise financial systems, plan expenditures and give accurate reports in detail.   Notice his balanced reserved style, the logical connections, equal spacings and orderly marginal alignment. This writer would approach any industrial proposition, or any other, calmly, with an inward eye trained to dis-

This, it seems to me, is an exal as it will enable the Commissi more intelligently in deciding:

No. 15

cover errors and rectify mistakes. He indites, as you see, a cool, rounded hand with his small letters pointed at the top; while his lines are straight—honesty—and his equally moderately low words—attention to details with the penetration to see a final solution to any problem which presents itself.

Also he would be systematic to the last degree. Were his figures present you would note instantly their copper-plate appearance. With

the times given are well written possible and easy. fulfilment

No. 16

what care he places his punctuation. People who are allied to this in these pen-particulars are adapted for accountancy, auditing, statistical engineering and the most exacting mathematical calculations.

Thus with No. 16 evidences of like character are shown, with one exception worthy of consideration. This writer's curved and rigid swing would make him over-diligent and too conscientious, if such is possible. He writes straight without any gross exaggerations in the way of muddied formations. He is the type who would work under the electric light far into the night—and perhaps miss his train. If this points a moral all well and good. But where figures must be accurate, balances at the end of the day correct, then it is poor policy for any firm to instal a system that makes for overwork. The writer shows loyalty and a willingness to assume even the smallest responsibilities. This is where this man is less efficient than that preceding.

THE SCIENTISTS AND ENGINEERS

As the spheres of endeavor are many, so the types which disclose a scientific and engineering trend are many. Still No. 17 possesses the pen traits which are in common with those who are masters of commercial and other forms of engineering. Here stand out clearly the

No. 17

regular positive flow, decided pressure, semi-angular, with each stroke well defined and clean cut. Logic, reason, clarity of thought and lancet-like perceptions are this individual's endowments. His low, small, acute letters jointly help this writer to make keen cutting analyses and gives an intense power of application. These qualities of mind in combination show that any mathematical problem would be easy to

4

solve, any system to give the best results in the shortest time would be readily effected.

And here again, if you saw his figures, you would remark that they were made in a sort of offhand manner. Not those of an accountant.

refer me to any good book on the

always been interested in handwriting

No. 18

These are the leading signs used by efficiency experts apart from the angle in which the words are written. For the slant has nothing to do with a man's or woman's scientific ability.

It is readily recognized that No. 18 was inscribed by a person where extreme care, precision and exactitude in writing are prominent features. The low letters are made in a mechanical fashion, while the acuteness betrayed is the revelation of a man with a diacritical eye which penetrates below the surface and reaches the actual facts which supply

No. 19

scientific proof. Such writers devote their energies to electricity, biology and cognate subjects. In fact any one can recall that Thomas A. Edison displays these inky characteristics. These letters bear a strong resemblance to print.

The curvilinear style of No. 19 flaunts an intellect and tendencies which would be active in any field of work except science. So it behooves the wise employer to select for positions where a scientific bent, routine and minute investigation are the requisites only such writing which is devoid of such excessive curves and will show like indications as referred to above.

ANALYZING THE EDITORS

Turning to the field where editorial capacity is indicated—and the types are most abundant—exhibits Nos. 20 and 21 show the chief

No. 20

hallmarks pointing to efficiency in this widely maligned line of work. Notice that, though quite individual in form and style, still both possess marked continuity of thought, alert, observant minds with the ability for large conceptions, and fine, critical faculties.   Here are the

No. 21

fleet swing, the pointed small letters, with the strokes of long letters leaping high above the base lines.   Rare discrimination appears.

Excellent judgment stands revealed by the balanced spaces. There are the stiletto-like "d's" and "t's"—signs of an unerring mental touch in making a choice.

The first one has a wider range of vision than the second. He sees his objective and flies right to it. The second is more deliberate and would weigh public opinion in many instances too long. Each is given the endowment of artistic taste. Each shades the down and cross strokes to some extent, the infallible indication of responsiveness to all impressions, to all emotions. But it is an intellectual or sensuous responsiveness. And the more pronounced these are, omitting the temperamental and emotions indications, the greater the editorial ability, pure and simple.

Publishers, take notice. Editor, also, if you please.

Now there are stenographers and stenographers! Nevertheless, it is interesting to find that No. 22, with her constant lively pen prints,

No. 22

her straight base lines and small letters of nearly even height, closely reaches the peak of sincerity, straightforwardness, diligence, honesty and industry. True she possesses curves, but it indicates a willing disposition and an accommodating manner in taking dictation after 5.30.

OFFICE BOY NOT FORGOTTEN

Surely we must not forget the office boy, who may be a prospective financier. In the employment of office boys one must consider the adolescent muscles, half dreams. However, in the case of No. 23, on account of his rapid, sharp style, his high and positive "t" bars and fairly even pressure he is the sort who would tackle his work with

No. 23

diligence, show an intelligent mind, be observant and inclined to orderliness.

"God bless us! Is this possible?" you say.

Yes, his script rushes ahead—restlessness. But note especially his clear though slightly variable punctuation. Later such a writer with encouragement would handle the files correctly and see that letters were mailed on time.

"Good heavens!"

Again yes. And certainly you do not wish for laziness and stupidity. So beware of the extreme backhand, with heavy, rather muddy writing and a changeable base line when you seek for a reliable boy.

In this connection it may be said that apparently numerous exceptions will be found to those described heretofore. Still, close examination of these exhibits will furnish definite and accurate clues for the selection of such associates as will prove reliable and desirable as the years go by.

To employ individuals without the psychological test is liable, as it has been shown many times to be an expensive proposition in commercial life as well as elsewhere. Unlike other methods, the signs appearing take on the reflections of mind, body and soul. And to make a correct interpretation requires a study of men's and women's *tout ensemble*, collectively and individually.

We are approaching a new era in the business world, and this era is that of common sense. If I were a statistician I would wonder how many of the readers are gifted with this trait.

CHAPTER IV

REPRESENTATIVE MEN IN THE UNITED STATES

REPRESENTATIVE men in the United States of America display predominant features in various forms and lines of endeavors.

No. 1.   Steady energy, determination, with the ability to formulate big conceptions.   Positive in holding his ideas in toto.   Diplomacy is shown by the strong final extension of the last strokes of his signature.

No. 2.   With one stroke of his pen he declares his rapid mental processes.   Virile, keen, accurate, resourceful and daring.   Power of resistance.   A director of men.

No. 3.   Calm, cool, deliberate.   Self-contained and always using to advantage his intellectual powers.   His mind controls his emotions. Emphasizing his lofty ideas as shown by his very high capitals.

No. 4.   Strength, purpose, keenness, powers of observation and
geniality. Sure of his motives and beliefs. Self-poised with initiative.
Tactful under all situations.   Capable.

No. 5.   Mental powers are in the ascendant, a vigorous imagination with receptivity to ideas. Positive of his convictions, but not
opinionated.   Fluency of language shown by steady flow.   Kind,
sympathetic and adaptable to all conditions.   Frank, generous, and a
mixer with men.   Personality is unique.

No. 6.   Rapid in thought and action, dominant, sure of his ground.
Capable of analysis and proficient in making close deductions.   Positive
executive ability.

Frank A. Munsey

No. 7.   Decided, firm, energetic, with a keen, alert mind.   Will to achieve is ever present.   He knows his own powers, exhibiting the result-producing backward stroke under his signature.

M. G. Scheopp.

No. 8.   A positive, emphatic nature, with decisions made by accuracy and definiteness.   Convincing, thorough and to the point.   Self-assurance, control and will power are evident.

Henry R. Towne.
9 Murray St.

No. 9.   Mental and physical equipoise, initiative, good judgment and calculation.   Ambition is emphasized by firmness.

Francis L. Leland

No. 10.   Keen perception, shrewdness, perseverance, with large ideas.   Practical and independent.   Adaptable to people and usually tactful.   Reserved but agreeable.

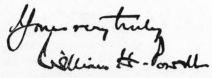

No. 11.   Poise, determination, ability to weigh the pros and cons.
Analytical, skillful, resourceful, systematic, with a master hand at
details.   Executive sense reinforced by calm judgment.   Fairness and
justice.

No. 12.   Marked continuity of thought, caution, self-control and
reserved power.   Perseverance, vigilance and fortitude.   Imagination
is practical.

No. 13.   Daring, frank, enthusiastic, thinks quickly, with keenness and shrewdness.   Handles affairs to the smallest detail.   Strong,
generous, aggressive character.

No. 14.   Great powers of concentration, continuity of thought,
ability to arrive at decisions.   Intellectually aggressive, with caution.
Critical and quietly enthusiastic.   Modest, frank, and generous.   Facts
appeal scientifically.

No. 15.   Strength of purpose.   Directness in action, quick mental
powers, independence and perseverance.   Optimism and physical
buoyancy combined with courage.   A dominant man.

No. 16.   Powerful reasoning faculties, clear vision, foresight and
perfect application.   Balance, patience, coolness in emergencies.
With courage, self-esteem and mastery of himself.

Princeton, N.J. April 19, 1922.

Dear Sir:

This is a specimen of my handwriting today. Yesterday it was better. Tomorrow it may be worse. In the next life I hope it will be much improved.

Sincerely yours,

Henry van Dyke.

To
Mr. William Leslie French.

No. 17.   Intellectual faculties are highly developed; imagination, reasoning powers and perception.   Cheerfulness, loyalty, patience and sense of responsibility and belief in himself. Courtesy and tact. Originality in formulating ideas. Modest and retiring. Ideality.

Yours very truly,

No. 18.   Cool, deliberate, balanced, reasonable and careful.   Decided and dogmatic. Independent, and uses calculation. Is vigilant and confident. Strong force of character.

Harrington Emerson

No. 19. Perseverance, energy, aggressiveness, liveliness, with great optimism. Idealistic but practical. Mind works rapidly with great concentration. Fluency in speech and promoting ideas. No vanity but much esteem. Pleasing and agreeable, but demands to accomplish his purposes. Personality plus!

No. 20. Fleet mental action, buoyancy, and quick to take advantage over conditions. Looks for results and is accurate in attaining them. Always is able to control associates.

No. 21. Force, constancy to his ideas, alertness, and patient in working towards his own ends. Tact and courtesy and amenable to reason. His mind is never still. So he employs every resource ambitiously. He is efficient to 98 per cent.

No. 22. The writer has a good disposition, has advanced ideas and he thinks clearly. Has speed and accuracy, fortitude and responsiveness. Adapts himself in a cheerful fashion. Reasonable.

[signature: Sam'l Untermyer]

No. 23. Intellectual honesty, deliberate in actions, cautious and dogmatic in his conceptions. Never stops until he secures his end. Plans and executes. A man with ambitious ideas. Energetic to the *nth* degree.

[signature: Sincerely, Bion J. Arnold]

No. 24. The ability to accomplish results, with a clear, active brain and endurance is plain. Imagination is scientific. Quick thought animates every motive and plan. Common sense is powerful.

[signature: Now is the winter of our discontent made glorious summer etc. Thos A Edison]

No. 25. Logic, clarity of ideas, perceptions and fine analytical insight. Deductions. Definitely under control and never moved from his stand. His words are similar to figures. His signature is inventive in form.

149 BROADWAY.

My Dear Mr. French — I am not so sure that I ought to submit my character to this very baffling test without reserving the right of cross-examination. Anyhow my handwriting changes so much with my humours or pre-occupation that I could formulate a very good defence; I am quite convinced that — at times — I write a very "good hand" and yet in half a dozen ink spots & smudges — at all events this is a fair sample of daily performance

Very truly,

No. 26. There is a virile intellect which guides every movement, an audacious determination combined with courage. Strong opinions are thought out and tenacity is the foundation. The hand movement of his signature means strength.

Among this distinctive group are men who have shown signal service in one capacity or another. But their script-formations stand forth, reflecting in each instance as unique and characteristic. So it is sufficient for them to declare their caliber, without any further word that I can say.

T. Roosevelt

No. 27.

I yield to no one in my love of Peace and my hatred of War.

Beverly

Sept. 9th 1912.

Wm H Taft

No. 28.

...fail now to show the world for what their wealth was intended.

Woodrow Wilson

No. 29.

No. 30.

No. 31.

No. 32.

No. 33.

No. 34.

THE SECRETARY OF WAR,

WASHINGTON.

October 2, 1917

My dear Mr. French:

I shall be interested to compare your deductions from the handwriting of the men whose personalities are known to me by intimate association, with the impressions which I already have of them.

Sincerely yours,

Newton D. Baker.

Mr. William Leslie French,
City Island,
N. Y.

No. 35.

Very sincerely yours

Irving Fisher

No. 36.

Yours very truly

Edward N. Hurley

No. 37.

Liberty" supreme throughout the World.

W. G. McAdoo

No. 38.

It isn't money alone that draws
men on to great enterprise; it is
that glowing satisfaction that
comes from fine achievement.

C M Schwab

No. 39.

Believe me, with many thanks,

Most truly yours

Daniel C. French.

No. 40.

CHAPTER V

THE ADMINISTRATION X-RAYED

An Analysis from The Handwritings of the Men Who Rule in Washington

THE American people in November 1920 made an important direct investment in the character and personality of Mr. Warren G. Harding and an important contingent investment in those of Mr. Calvin Coolidge. But apart from what we know of his words and acts, apart from

No. I

the impression which his portrait or his presence has made upon us, what do we, the American people, know about the real man—Mr. Harding? Or about Mr. Coolidge?

Or about Mr. Harding's coadjutors—the members of his Cabinet—who, the product of his own selection, are in a sense a projection of his personality?

Actually we know little, and under the circumstances this is natural. Still, by careful attention to one small act, the movement of Mr.

Harding's hand and pen in writing, we can get into closer touch with his personality than by any other means short of sharing his daily life. Today handwriting is generally accepted as an accurate guide to character, intellectual endowment and consequent behavior. As an interpreter of this sign-language I will invite you, therefore, to use your eyes and mind in following the President's pen prints; those of Mr. Coolidge, too, and those also of the members of the Cabinet, in an effort to gauge more exactly the value of that vitally important investment made on Election Day.

Mr. Harding's signature is outstanding in individuality. Every man who has shown by his acts any special distinction, throws a particular force and directness into his holograph which sets him in one way or another above his fellowmen. So with Mr. Harding!

The distinguishing features are his steady, even pressure, firm, positive, direct flow, with every connecting stroke between words well-made, giving his signature one unbroken movement. Here appear the vital evidence of a strong intellect, a dominant method of formulating ideas, an ability to plan and execute, without harshness, but with steady purpose and quiet determination.

He does not hesitate when he once makes up his mind. He reasons closely, but is not a calculating logician. He is not a scientist, but a certain deft insight and excellent judgment are emphasized by his perfect marginal alignment on the left and the sharpened formation to be found throughout.

He always fights with suavity, a genial disposition and diplomacy as weapons. And gets there! The movement is round and flowing! He has vision, but is not driven by his imagination. No superlative gestures of pen. His eyes are wide open to any and all possibilities, and he is wise enough to realize that he does not know it all. That is what his capital letters proclaim.

He is the most patiently impatient man! Note his t-bars. Almost every action has for its base a deep-rooted sentiment. Those who come in contact with him intimately know that he is a generous man, endowed with a generosity which prevents his ever becoming an implacable foe. Still he has a canny eye and a canny mind, curiously suspicious.

In all-round efficiency—considering that he is neither an expert nor a human dynamo—I place him close to 96 per cent. The other 4 per cent. represents an odd kind of languor—shall I say laziness?—peculiarly his own!

It is not a matter for wonderment that Mr. Harding has invited Mr. Coolidge to act in an advisory capacity to the Chief Executive—something new in the lot of a Vice-President. But in view of Mr.

No. 2

Harding's keen judgment of men, Mr. Coolidge's signature thus exhibited will afford an additional reason for the departure. It was penned by a personality marked by a quiet, persistent reserve—amounting almost to diffidence—coupled with a discriminating mind, keen powers of observation and a steady propensity for absorbing facts. His angles and triangles indicate that he approaches in a scientific attitude any proposition. He is cold, alert and calculating, not given to superabundant speech. He is an analyst and moves slowly. Those associated with him constantly will find that he does not lack nerve.

He is the type that would not shirk a responsibility, for he is rigid in his attitude towards what he believes his duty. His capitals and fine-pointed style show that in the final analysis he could impale those who attempted to be underhanded. Still, he has that common sense which permits others to state their side before he acts. Just! Despite his reserve, he has a big self-confidence when it comes to handling large affairs. His stubbornness is intellectual. He is capable of harmonizing his point of view to meet conditions and individuals, but will ever reserve his own right to his opinion—and give it quietly, though not without fact.

As he lifts his curved and tri-angular C's, so in all matters of importance he has that sort of vision which is stimulated by actual self-confidence. He is practical, and can be counted on to play his hand intelligently—and according to Hoyle. The sum total of his strokes reveals a rather unique personality.

Were Mr. Hughes a Frenchman, one might say that his intellectual processes were divided—like all Gaul—into three parts. But being an American, his lack of extreme subtlety and finesse merely modifies his

No. 3

mental action so that he becomes a composite intellectuality. His calm, semi-vertical, poised script, reinforced by large capitals, proclaims equipoise, deliberation, and caution. A man of broad ideas, unlimited as to scope, you can be assured that he always approaches a subject in a broad way first, and then like a surgeon applies his critical analytical faculty to cut away any and all fallacies. There is an angularity in several portions, which endows him with a tenacity in presenting his views—an intensity in forcing his convictions, which are always CONVICTIONS!

He is fair and just, and though able to quibble, will not. He has a certain curvature of the script, but not of the spine or disposition. Emphatic!

You will observe that his base-line wavers slightly, an indication that he will evade committing himself before weighing every iota of evidence. He evidently has a way of quietly smiling away a compliment, due to an ironic sense of humor, which also prevents him from showing irritation at human flies and mosquitoes. But there is a vein of mental irritability if obstacles are placed in the way of carrying out his policies.

The deft fashion of turning a word or phrase is the result of his acute mind. He reminds one of an eagle, keen-eyed in viewing the landscapes of the world, ever ready to swoop down, when the occasion warrants, upon an enemy. Resourcefulness and dignified action are high lights of his personality.

Now, Mr. Hoover's script-forms serve as an excellent letter of introduction to the fact that he is typically American because he never

No. 4

knows when he is beaten. His rapid, free-flowing movement, minutely wrought words and letters, well-connected, sharpened at the top, signify fleet thinking, fleet acting, instant decisions, with application to the smallest details, as well as the ability to supervise.

If you once stacked up against this writer in an argument or a discussion you would find that he was well-nigh invincible in his firmness. His lower strokes—the y—descend like a hammer for force. Yet his ending of words is lower than their beginning—a diplomatic tendency which modifies the flow. But in his slow anger, his indignation, he is massive in assault. He can be exceedingly abrupt. His finals are as reserved as he is. Yet this does not interfere with his candor or actual sincerity.

His vision and imagination are untrammeled by what people think. In fact, when his mind is concentrated upon his work, he forgets everything else. But he is unsparing of himself, and will spare others. He is considerate and approachable, if you know how. A man of courage and of nerve! His nerves are taut under the whip of his brain, lashing to accomplishment. Afterwards, extreme flexibility.

He is absolutely unafraid to take chances, risks, and gamble against the highest odds. He is a man with a hunch that he is right. The sharp dash under his signature is the keynote to his personality—the determination to get things done!

"There shall be wars and rumors of wars," saith the Scriptures, and Mr. Weeks, the Secretary of War, exhibits a mailed fist as far as his cool determination, enterprise and practical common sense are con-

No. 5

cerned. That he has steady insistence and the will to put into effect his plans are indicated by the forceful pressure, the sharpened style and high capitals. Combined with shrewdness is intellectual poise.

He is not one who would lose control over his subordinates, and he is one who would deal with each problem which came under his supervision with thorough efficiency. In fact, he surveys what he has to accomplish with a cool eye and head devoid of that imagination which would lead him to regard facts as anything else but facts. In consequence he is rather frank, outspoken, and hearty in the expression of his opinions, even though they may hit hard and plenty. His self-assurance enables him always to stand on both feet. Like his bold signature, he goes out to accomplish things, and will not use silk gloves to attain his purposes.

He moves across the page in a comfortable fashion, showing nothing erratic. He takes things easily. His is a genial though bluff handwriting.

Especially marked is his strength, which contributes to his power of endurance. Note the vigor shown by the long extension of the J below the line. As he takes himself seriously, he expects others to so regard him. His personality is forceful and dignified.

In vivid contrast, Mr. Hays, the man with a mile-a-second mind, works with a speed which is reflected in his intense virile, nervous, alert writing. His energy flows from the tips of his fingers, his quick-

No. 6

ness, alertness, and positive way of crossing his t's and dotting his i's, is reinforced by the large lasso formation over capital w's—confidence supreme in his ideas, his plans!

His whole style is glowing with temperament, the kind which makes itself felt in all transactions, with all individuals. His gift of speech, even of staccato insistence at times, is the result of a live, vigorous imagination, a fleet vision. He is an individual who will take the initiative to the *nth* degree, and the greater the odds the better he seems to work.

Observe his pointed small letters and the original dashes he uses for periods. His discretion and caution are heavenly twins, for he follows his hunch and follows naturally, with both these holding the reins tautly.

He is the type who enjoys besting an opponent just for the keen excitement of the game. As his base-line swings along unevenly, so he takes pleasure in keeping people guessing. And withal frank, talkative, with an abundant humor. He will never be satisfied unless on the jump, unless he can originate new schemes and ideas. He understands details, but hates them. He likes to supervise in a large fashion.

There are those who hit the bull's-eye by steady, restrained efforts, controlled impulses, calmness, and easy deliberation, and the handwriting of Mr. Davis falls in this class. His decisions are animated, and

No. 7

put into effect by careful thought and consideration, and he never will attempt to coerce by dominant aggressive brutality. He holds that you can catch more flies with molasses than vinegar—one who will compromise but not yield when the issue is great.

He has tact, a quiet sort of diplomacy, and will meet everyone halfway at least. He has the courage of his opinions, but waits to hear the views of those with whom he associates. He has a mathematical and precise mind, dealing with each problem which confronts him cautiously and even slowly. His power of adaptation is marked. He makes no effort to antagonize, but will occasionally show a curious persistency.

He holds to a straight forward course of action, but reserves his opinion—until later. You will note the rather large, comparatively firm hand, lofty capitals, and carefully formed words, each final extending outward with a sweep. He shows a good deal of sympathy even to those with whom he may be at odds.   He will be good-natured and deal kindly, having a broad way of looking at things, situations and problems.   There is no evidence in this specimen that he is very analytical.   One who likes details as a hobby.

There is a high degree of natural sensitiveness coupled with much personal pride.   His ambition is unflagging.   He is not a bold originator of schemes, but conservative, following along safe lines.   Essentially a man who takes the *via media* both socially and in public life.   One to whom family and friends are meat and drink.   His personality is quiet and unassuming.

Mr. Mellon's minute, delicately poised characters, firm and distinctive, give an important and valuable clue to his mental processes.   His

No. 8

chief endowment is his active, analytical, discriminating mind.   It is as if he had bound himself by certain scientific limitations, exact and perfectly defined.

The almost microscopic size of his handwriting reflects his enormous power of application.   Accurate, sure and meticulously careful, he measures his words, his actions with the same care that he does the spacings between his words and letters.   Not a superlative curve or flourish!   No flamboyant imagination!   He deals with actualities, facts, and he permits himself to be guided by them only.   A close calculator, a rigid estimator!   From the practical point of view, almost a machine. But the angle at which he writes and his rounded flow also show that he is extremely human, agreeable and has much sentiment.

He is impatient and particular, precise, punctual.   Emphatic in his decisions, he brings his down strokes below the line, bluntly, as though to make clear his yea or nay.   Foresight, insight, shrewdness and clear vision are his, for he never moves until he is positive of his own position. He is intrigued by big transactions, large deals, important measures, and can play his hand skillfully. But he is far from adamant.

It is well that his understanding of human motives is keenly developed, for he is not affected by too much suavity or influenced against his will.

As an all-round example of tense but characteristic unhaste, he stands forth preëminent. His signature displays a kindly dignity.

There is a saying of old that "Wisdom is justified of her children," and the truth of this is exemplified by the distinctive signature, unique in formation—written by Mr. Daugherty. His practically vertical style, uniform pressure, excellent connections, with small letters pointed at the top, show that he is wise, has a long head, clear and keen per-

No. 9

ceptions allied with a broad vision as to practical affairs. He possesses the will to achieve and cannot be swerved from his purpose. That is what he means by making his t-bar of such marked size and ending in a club. He would employ an immense amount of energy and virile persistence to accomplish his ends. But to those associated with him, this might not be apparent, because he has a silent suavity, a diplomatic method which works admirably. Observe how he lowers his small letters with a slope to the right.

When he throws his strokes pointedly high above the line he calls attention to the fact that his ability to look ahead, to advise others to see what the future can bring forth, has the quality of prophecy. He understands how to adapt himself to circumstances, and he works with a certain kind of subtlety when necessary. Not a man who talks unnecessarily—but to the point.

The dominant features of Mr. Wallace's mental composition are his deliberate fashion of working out his problems, emphasized by intense power of concentration, and a logical mind. His steady hand reflects a steady brain. Viewing slowly, even cautiously, the conditions which prevail, the intricate interlocking causes which affect the interests that

very sincerely

Henry C. Wallace

No. 10

feed the nation, he makes his plans with every detail worked out to the smallest iota. For he is not a visionary man, but one who, though he may have comprehensive ideas, does not flaunt them abroad, until he is sure of his ground.

His pen-movement is carefully guided slightly upwards to the right, capitals moderately high, in proportion to his small letters, which are very low. There is no dash or flourish about him. His wisdom lies in his conclusions, in his willingness to accept new ideas and suggestions without feeling any antagonism. Or if he feels that any attitude is hostile, he keeps his mouth closed. With him, "Shut mouths catch no flies," and he will express his opinion with skillful caution.

If you chanced to interview him and get a statement of his policies, you would find that he is agreeable, rather reserved, somewhat evasive. He will wait on your move before he enters into any details as to his plans. In fact, he is a good waiter.

As an executive, he will be apt to consider details of paramount importance, of utmost necessity, and his decisions will perhaps bring forth criticism on account of his unusual care. His power of reconstruction is, with the few words he has written, less in evidence than his ability to get at the root of any trouble.

From the virility, strength, rapidity and force of his handwriting, you can readily see that Mr. Fall needs no spur to rowel him into action. For his writing abounds in all the hallmarks of the man who knows his own course of action and will adhere to it, despite obstacles or objections. The connections are well-made, but often there are breaks which indicate that his mind works without special oiling and that he arrives at his decisions with almost instant vision. Of course

[handwritten note] Pressure of official business is my excuse for this tardy answer,
Sincerely yours
Albert B. Fall

No. 11

there are the impatient dashes, the pointed tops of his small letters—symbolical of the fact that he will fight for what he thinks is right, and take no back-talk from anybody.

And yet, after all, he can be tactful, and understands the value of harmony.

He grasps details and also has a synthetical side which enables him to recognize faults and leaks in his department and to remedy them so that the various branches will work toward one common efficient end. And he means what he says when he gives an order.

His intellect takes the quality of scientific investigation. But his is the practical way of looking at affairs, not the visionary, although he possesses that imagination which stimulates to what is feasible and possible in the future.

There is every indication of a temperament, which causes him to feel any adverse criticism keenly. Further, his sense of right, of the proper things to do at the proper time, his firm convictions, all give him a deep realization of responsibility.

He is approachable, but always in a hurry, naturally. Still he has tough self-restraint to cover this tendency under normal conditions.

Ambition reinforced by a far-sighted policy as to results as to the value of firmness and decisive action are marked features, all pointing to the fact that he holds up his head as an American citizen—decidedly.

About a thousand years B. C. "King Solomon made a navy of ships on the shore of the Red Sea," and by his supervision this navy brought him fame. And to the same and the signature of Mr. Denby with his

No. 12

heavy pressure, virile, strong contours and bold lofty capitals, expresses his real skill. He thinks forcibly, even massively, and being dead sure of his own convictions and his opinions, he acts—and acts with cold, steel-like firmness.

His high extensions above and below the line reflect his dignity, his belief in dignified action, in not going to extremes except in some great emergency. Despite any adverse criticism, he will stand pat, and stand! He is more or less stubborn and has marked power of resistance. Hence, he cannot be forced actually to do anything against his will.

His is a practical mind, logical in its processes, with ideas of efficiency highly developed. Not an imaginative man who jumps just because he has a new idea. He will weigh the evidence and then render his decision. His sense of justice will cause him to enforce discipline even if he wishes to do the opposite—a statement which may be taken generally or specifically.

Now in view of the foregoing regarding the script formations of these twelve individuals, we find that taken separately each is a silent force, but that together they form a *tour de force*, moving quietly, and in most instances conservatively, to definite achievement. When we consider that to these men is entrusted the control of a nation whose power, wealth and influence are unsurpassed in history, the fact that they reflect that degree of caution, if only collectively, should give their co-partners—the American people—a certain amount of confidence in the value of their investment.

The signature of an individual is a reflection in miniature of his personality, but like all small things which count in this world, it counts, and counts large.

CHAPTER VI

STANDARD FORMS OF EXECUTIVES

THEIR leading pen-traits are easily recognized, significant of special abilities. The handwriting is always forceful, energetic, well-balanced, with connections well made. The capitals are large, high, but in proportion to the small letters.

No. 1.   Administrative Ability.

No. 2.   Bank Executive.

No. 3.   Director of Banking Interests.

No. 4.   Bank Executive Financier.

No. 5.   Bank Director Diplomatist.

No. 6.   Engineering Executive.

No. 7.   Financial Director.

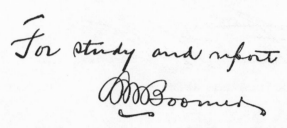

No. 8.   Executive Manager.

No. 9.   Comptroller.

No. 10.   Executive Bank Accountant,

No. 11.   Secretarial Executive.   (a)

No. 12.   Secretarial Executive.   (b)

No. 13.   Educational Executive.

No. 14.   Promotor-Executive.

In the administration of justice there are numerous forms found, but they can be accepted as authoritative. The signs most easily noted are virile connections, with the writing poised and sharpened at the top.

No. 15.   Executive Judge.

No. 16.   Executive Jurist.

CHAPTER VII

COMMERCIAL TYPES

In the class of Managers, Salesmanagers, and Advertising Executives are writers whose script-signs are very similar. Observe that there is a firm, flowing, rounded style, sometimes vertical, but the writing is not very low. The capitals are usually twice the size of the small letters. Where many flourishes abound, then also is self-importance and conceit. When the long letters extend quite above the line, a big commercial imagination is in evidence. Strong, steady writing emphasizes a person's ability to influence others tactfully and convincingly. Those following are typical of those who understand management and are able to sell successfully.

No. 1. Advertising Executive.

Philip Robbé

No. 2.   Advertising Executive and Salesman.

Yours very sincerely

T. Wackewitz.

No. 3.   Office Salesmanager.

addressed — to me personally

Frank S. Evett.

No. 4.   General Salesmanager.

to co-operate

you. Yours very truly

N. B. Hatch

No. 5.   Salesmanager, Salesman.

Wm G. Sengel

No. 6.   Managing Editor.

RICHARD H. WALDO
119 WEST 40TH STREET
NEW YORK CITY

21 Apl '22

Dear Mr. French:-

From the days when you taught Sunday school to now I have admired your work - Good luck to its newest phase.

Very sincerely

Richard H. Waldo.

No. 7.   Circulation Manager.

Advertising has become in ree years a dominant factor in a commercial life

[signature] Shaun Presbrey

No. 8.   Advertising Director.

The joining link between managerial ability and that of salesmanship is a close one.   Managers are usually recruited from the sales force. Salesmen have similar pen-strokes who are able.   The uniform firm swing, with quite tightly closed writing and rather high looped extensions above the lines.   Imaginative faculty, but controlled!   Always the energetic type.

some business, three years and a half overseas.

No. 9.   Salesman.

With kindest regards.

Sincerely Yours.

[signature] Nigel Blackmurley-Jones.

No. 10.   Advertising Specialist.

Broadway

New York City —

No. 11.   Salesman.

very sincerely, your

Adolf Browski.

No. 12.   Sales Specialist in Designs.

Yours very truly,

F. M. Turner

No. 13.   Sales Specialist in Art Lines.

The choice of reliable employees who have business capacity, able to serve in the accounting departments, handle figures accurately, as credit men shrewd, responsible, all these belong to a certain handwriting class.   The script is medium in height, legible, neat, margins even with equal spaces between words and lines.   Punctuation exact. High capitals accentuate confidence and ability.   Too many flourishes betray conceit.   When the writing is pointed at the top, keenness and suspicion are indicated.

I enclose you $10.00 for one as above

Yours Very Truly

OFEUnderhill

No. 14.   Expert Accountant.

*present engaged as a book-
desire to become a salesman.*

No. 15.   Bookkeeper.

*in exchange your will
to prepare this check.*

particular hurry and

No. 16.   General Auditor.

Very truly yours,

Mildred E. Pittman

No. 17.   Secretary.

May success always be yours.

J. Edw. McCula—

No. 18. Credit Man.

CHAPTER VIII

DETECTING DISHONESTY

Traits of Criminals of All Types Stand Out Clearly in Their Pen-Strokes—How One Was Startled Into a Remarkable Confession.

IT was the hour between 6 and 7, the usual period of relaxation for those who were participating in the allied bazaar which was being held in a large auditorium in New York. The occupant of a booth situated on the main aisle casually glanced upward as a tall, well groomed man sauntered by. He hesitated slightly and then stopped, reading a printed announcement.

"That individual has been frequenting this spot every afternoon and evening," he mused. "He looks like a clubman or a cosmopolitan financier." The next instant the stranger came nearer and questioned in a well modulated voice: "What is this special line of work, may I ask?"

"Psychological interpretation from handwriting," the script psychologist answered. "Write a few words in your natural hand with the initials and date and I will tell you what you are, your motives and probable actions." He did not lift his eyes as he spoke, but beckoned to a chair opposite. Even then the man waited, but finally sat down and wrote a few lines. The expert looked up. Eyes met eyes, the one penetrating and half-questioning, the other cold, expressionless and inscrutable. Each betrayed a poker face.

"Do you wish me to tell you everything, just as I see it? The whole unvarnished truth? I do not mince words and am brutally frank—always."

The other nodded, emphasizing his assent with a brief movement of his long, slender hand.

"YOU ARE A CROOK!"

Scanning the strong, decided abbreviated style for a moment from the left side, and again inverting the specimen, he glanced down at the initials of the signature. He paused, his gaze fixed on a point distant. "You are a natural, perverse, calculating crook. You lie cleverly," he said. "You are cold and hard and do not hesitate to fleece every one with whom you come in contact, if you consider it worth while. With a mind and nerves like steel, you are very persuasive and cautious! You——"

"Go on," his client put in evenly.

"You always play for big stakes and you have no use for a piker. Once a man or woman double crosses you, and a lifetime would only be too short until you had your revenge. Every indication points to your real occupation—a gambler!" A simultaneous flash of equal interest darted between them. "But you often prove yourself to be a generous friend."

"Do I like women?" he stilettoed back.

"No. Once you might have. Yet with you all men lie."

The large heavily lidded eyes of the man opposite glared balefully. Then a charming smile lit his face. With a changed inflection, he remarked, in a suave tone. "You are dead right, in every particular. Like King David, who said in his haste 'All men are liars,' so I say deliberately all men and women lie, for love or money, or both. Still, where, may I inquire, do you find all that? Not surely in my few pen scratches. But how could you possibly know otherwise!" He picked up his written specimen, with a curious, detached air, peering at this replica of his personality.

"Damn! Eh—pardon me, Mr. Psychologist, I would not have you

7

around me constantly for even—a belief in humanity. What shows my professional tendency and assumed success?" His thin lips widened into a partial sneer.

"Why, the slight wavy base line almost imperceptible, the fine small letters pointed at the top, these being unequal in height and close together, and your short finals and finished style."

"You certainly get down to the facts, don't you? Well, it is worth the money to hear the whole truth, sometimes, when stated from the impersonal point of view. You forgot to say that I never indulge in confidences.'

"Pardon me," he threw back. "Your a's and o's are so tightly formed that they catch no flies, as the Spanish have it."

This little incident illustrative of the psychological surveying and measuring up of peoples' values, morals and actions opened the door to an acquaintance with many men and women whose methods of livelihood and manner of life are most attractive, I suppose, because irregular and not according to Hoyle.

So, if you will accompany me, I will show you a selected few who were friends of the friends of this "friend" the gambler, the man who in varied activities was until recent years a "man higher up." His holograph is interesting. His signature? Well, as he himself once said later on in our odd relationship: "Only a fool signs his real name."

As the desire to gamble, to take large risks or small, and to be actually dishonest, depend upon special innate qualities resident in certain people, it is readily seen that their tendencies and ultimate actions can be arrived at only through the appearance of a series of handwriting signs. The crafty crook displays his ingenuity, which is higher in degree than that of the common thief or pickpocket. He will show greater caution, shrewdness or finesse in achieving his ends as compared with a stoolpigeon who might be actually a coward at heart.

So, like two men whose noses are similar in shape, but one is sharper than the other, in the same manner their handwriting may reveal some hallmark which on account of its prominence or the reverse will set them far apart as regards their ability. And especially does this hold good with the members of the criminal fraternity!

When we seek for the men and women of the underworld who are skillful the signs of keen intelligence must naturally be first considered. And No. 1, which at first glance might have been inscribed by a Bishop with diplomatic executive ability, was penned by an astute, keenly intelligent, calculating, grasping crook whose machinations and

No. 1

manœuvres were so well planned that he could hold up the government as it were, to stand by and deliver. The rigidity of his down and cross strokes, with vital, forceful connections, unfold his intensely active mind and moral hardness.

But the deviation of the second line at the bottom and the rapid sharpening of his low letters at the top are bold symbols of ruse, cunning and utter deceit. He has the fine Machiavellian hand, able to worst his opponents by the most skillful knavery. Like my "friend," the man higher up? Yes. Is there a single letter open for inspection? A free, untrammeled stroke making for real human sympathy? There is not! This type has endless schemes to advance and puts them through. But keep silent!

Undoubtedly many a detective may disagree with these observations, only his eyesight and power of analysis might be defective, and having some client of this rank who did not write like this one may be peeved. And there you are.

A SENTIMENTAL CROOK

One would instantly remark that No. 2 is totally dissimilar to that preceding, both in pen-gait and, especially, the upward curving final strokes of some words—the sign of courage. Most certainly! The courage to rob a government of nearly a million dollars and get away with it. This nice old gentleman, with a smile as bland and fixed as

No. 2

Foxy Grandpa's, and his genial rounded script, was sentimental. He slants to the right at an angle of at least 45 degrees, and in consequence his deeply affectionate nature led him to confide in his stenographer, who carelessly left her a's and o's wide open above.

Naturally she had a near and dear friend who also talked. Thus, despite the writer's extreme caution and even usually deadly silence on financial matters, shown by the encircling stroke around the "Y" in "you," like the man who swallowed a cent had to pay ten dollars in interest to his physician, this writer was diplomatically informed that he had to make restitution. For in those good old days, High Finance did not trouble itself with any method like the psychology of hand-writing to gain protection.

By very close examination you will note the resembling signs of these two types of gamblers.

Likewise. No. 3 is groomed with the same kind of pen-clothing, although this specimen was written by one whose income would hardly warrant his being addicted to shady transactions. But in these days of

unquotable profiteering, his dividends diminish with his courage. As
he writes a weak hand and either short-stops his finals, or lets them drop

I am not in a position to subscribe to the stock…

No. 3

downward, he resorts to cunning and chicanery to get even with the
tax officials.

Observe how even his undulating base lines *lie*, and how he whittles
to a point his low letters uneven in height—craftiness! By these same
tokens he is devious in all of his methods, taking a delight naturally in
any deal. The undercurrent of excitement and high stimulation, for
he writes quickly with high extensions above the line, would rush this
person into the stock market and the race track. Big stakes, sweep-
stakes, or any stakes at all!

Of course, with these varied classes mentioned, there are numerous
other types connected, who rank from the clever, fascinating female spy
to the yegg man, the counterfeiter and others lower down in the scale
of questionable livelihood. So, in the acquisition of money when the
individual is given another impulse than straight avarice, or has mixed
motives and diverse inclinations. to boot, then the writing takes on
other forms which are distinct and have to be considered in order to
find the reasons why the crooked strain becomes predominant.

No. 4 reflects all the tendencies which impel the writer to seek for
luxury, coupled with a canny understanding, native buoyancy and
brilliancy. This was penned by a woman who belongs to the class
called spies. She was, and may be still, an internationalist. She has a
vivid personality, fascinating by her sheer vivacity and gift of language.
How rapidly she swings along with excellent and well-made connec-

No. 4

tions. Her hand inclines upward, as if to say, "Ah, there, my honey!" and never mean it.

PLEASURE IN DECEPTION

But she writes almost vertically in parts as well, significant of a shrewd mind actually in control, of cold calculation, of pleasure in deception. One look will convince that she also has the same signs of utter crookedness. She also adds the dashes of extreme caution after some of her words. Smile with a lie in her heart maybe, smile with a lie on her tongue just to secure what she temporarily craves—excitement, cards, luxury,—luxury always—and the hectic life. And her frequent slant with only one open at the top, the way that leads to her heart! One man only could really hold her, and for him she would sacrifice everything, would stop at nothing to get him wealth, even to the last throw. She stretches out the word "seen" and how great is her diplomacy! (A cosmopolitan hand.)

And it takes but the use of half an eye to see that No. 5 was written by an honest, clear thinking, clean-living woman. Many are these even though they vary somewhat in one pen-particular or another. Her script runs perfectly straight at the bottom, her pressure is uniform throughout, showing that her word is always good and that honor and sincerity are marked qualities. She is self-contained and does not go off into temperamental rages. She bars her t with decision while each

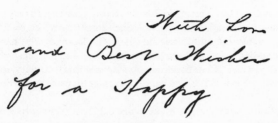

No. 5

extended final stroke inclining upward throbs with a deep sympathy and strong moral courage. A poised hand you say. Yes. And some contrast when you come to think of it!

> "Now man is something like a sausage,
> Very smooth upon the skin,
> But you can never tell exactly
> How much hog there is within."

Thus writes an observant cynic. Perhaps he did not consider that hoggishness is one powerful inclination prompting the individual to steal. The type abounds, alas!

In addition to his avarice, No. 6 by his distinct concentrated style, very low, small letters and cautious finals, proclaims his proficiency to

No. 6

think and act in devious, almost Oriental ways, and to plan under cover so effectually that others as well as himself may evade the law

Note that he, too, carries in his written aspect the display signs of craftiness and vulpine cleverness. Such might easily be some lawyer who frequents the capital of the State, the lobbyist who has a very understanding mind and a useful disposition. In such instances suspicion is justified of her children. And among this fraternity are others who write large and fulsome hands, but then they are not so especially gifted.

And here with Nos. 7, 8 and 9 are exhibited three types of stool-pigeons—first class as to efficiency, each one showing the dominant weakness which is at the root of their crookedness, the meanwhile ac-

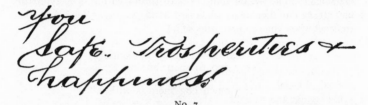

No. 7

centuating their inherited proclivities. Take No. 7. He reveals a straight hand apparently, plodding and almost print-like in its formation.

But his exceptionally heavy vulgar shading patched to the other strokes, flashlights his utter and uncontrolled desires for dissipation and vicious living. His curves are those of a dangerous beast, though quite intelligent. You can catch the scent in his pen regular irregularities. Sharp, his pin-pointed down-strokes below the lines bristle with hoggishness. Not one upward final stroke—detestable with moral cowardice! A lounge lizard or worse. One who would steal under direction whenever he had the opportunity. He is the kind who never travels alone, largely through fear.

His companion, No. 8, is more or less on the jump, more alert as appears in his fleet, somewhat jerky style. Yet, how weak are his words in their uncertain movement, in their occasional smudging!

He thinks quickly but with some hesitation. His t bars vary—his will
varies also. Some of his final strokes end in a hook, betraying a deft

*Oh the next morning what a sight
Would make anyone stop and think*

No. 8

hand which would fly into your pocket and out again with the contents,
instanter! This sign, even when considered alone, shows the possible
rabid collector of scarfpins and watches. A smooth article when it
comes to women! Easily influenced by minds and personalities cleverer
than his own.

Again, one would hardly think that the writing of No. 9, slow,
labored, sluggish and forced in its movement, even though comparatively regular and straight, is that of a man who under the influence of

*t is the art t
t o keep his b
l so that t
his Mind*

No. 9

a drug is swayed to dishonest actions. Naturally he has a slight tendency to dishonesty, but it was held in abeyance by other and stronger
traits. For instance, his clear t crossing which is still firm. There
remains a fragment of decency and honor, but it is almost submerged.

The sharp down stroke of "d" in "mind" discloses his irresolution, his fear. So, stimulated inclination has grown into a fiercely vicious state, which has brought him at last to live as a procurer, the lowest kind of thief. Degenerate in mind and body.

FEARLESS, BUT DEGENERATE

The connecting link between this writing and that of No. 10 seems very slight. However, both ply their nefarious trade, picking their

No. 10

gains from their victims regularly. But in the case of the latter, the wide-awake, alert, bold swing with its gross and heavy pressure signifies a man who will dare anything and everything to gain satisfaction. His tentacles, like the human devil-fish he is, are thrown out at the end of nearly every word to seize his prey, and having the ascendency, they will enslave these into oblivion.

A common type of the slave trader. One who is usually efficient until caught with the goods, and then he would crawl loathsomely, after he had made his first bluff. His is a confident handwriting. His advertising signs are the same as others. An odd trait is shown in his use of the Greek e, indicative of an intense love of beauty and a desire for material improvement, at least. An inherited tendency sign, without doubt.

In the last century there were '49ers who worked laboriously to attain wealth and affluence, which they spent with lavish hand. And the gold diggers of to-day, in large centres especially, employ their wits, "charm they never so wisely," adding to their loot from callow youth and senile "dementias" and aged gallants. That they dig with eye and voice, with other fascinations, is in part temperamentally depicted, in part incidentally, shown by illustrations Nos. 11 and 12.

No. 11

Here the first smiles coldly in her rapid flow, the even spacings between lines and excellent connecting strokes and cautious finals showing that she is a clever business woman. As she incarmines her lips, so heavily does her shading stand forth, announcing shamelessly her devotion to excessive luxuries, to foreign pleasures. Her wits are as sharp as her pointed low letters. Her desire is to gain, to spend, to spend and gain again, which she accomplishes without any compunction.

No. 12

CRAVES MONEY

The second through blinded folly and an intense overwrought imagination—see the wild erratic loops above the lines and a similar though varied application of ink—is frank in her desires for all that money will bring. She renders willingly unto Cæsar the things which Cæsar demands—if he will pay the price for a new mink or sable stole and muff.

But why pursue the twisted paths of these two, and others who write like them, any further? Electric lights under certain conditions produce blindness.

However, we can readily reserve our sympathy for No. 13, a woman who, by nature, possessed an active, clear mind, a bright intellect, but

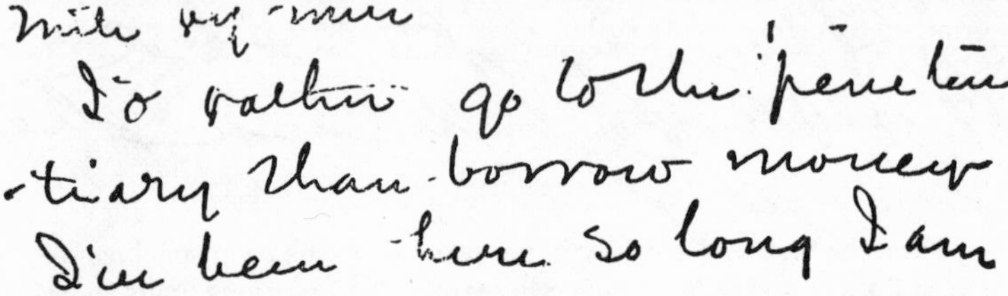

[handwritten sample]

No. 13

with an undercurrent of odd perversity which, through strain on the nervous system, became the dominant trait. She developed into a kleptomaniac, robbing right and left with apparently no control over her actions. She wrote this after she began to realize the peculiar twist in her make-up.

Consider how her script runs straight, and then varies with wavering lines. True, she is keen witted, as the pointed letter tops reveal. But these are to some extent exaggerated, becoming the symbols of cunning. She lies and then tells the truth with frankness. Her words are not written with an avaricious closeness, and selfishness is absent.

Under a lens there would appear a decided number of irregular quivers, some of which are visible to the naked eye. The depression of the lines at the right denote her bewilderment and melancholy. She realizes that she is face to face with a terrible situation. As an exhibit it is illuminating, and conveys how great a problem it is to determine the real motives of people, unless their physical states of mind and body are taken into consideration. Thus from observation and fine analysis it is discovered that kleptomaniacs have some disorder which is at the seat of their peculiarities.

To kite checks is a blamed nuisance to depositors and bank employees alike. Also to be able to pick out the writing of one who will tamper with his ledger, falsify and juggle accounts, is not the easiest thing in the world. For accurately to separate the distinctive signs of the types demands at least a discrimination in the use of words. To all intents, No. 14 inscribes a well poised hand, careful and exact, measuring up to a copperplate style. Yet this individual's greed and desire

will you be good enough to ascer. inform us, of the present address

No. 14

to get money and more money is reënforced by his finals, some abrupt and some absent. His intelligence and judgment are present, but back of these are the impulses to get all he can, no matter how. For the time he would be able to cover his defalcations. But, having an uneven and irregular pressure, he betrays his natural weakness of will and would break down when charged with his crime. He would be likely to overlook some minor detail—and he did. His vacation was limited to a term of several years. Not far sighted enough to be really efficient.

THE CHECK KITER

With No. 15 appears the type of man who, urged by his excitable nature and fiery conceit, thinks that he could make a killing in the stock market and get away with it. He would kite checks! The wild sweep of his looped letters on the first line displays his imagination running riot, especially as the other hallmarks of deviousness are found. Many of his letters hug themselves together as if they were chilled with the fear of loss. His finals curve high in the air, over-self-confidence and an inflation of his ideas.

Hence, with these tendencies, he finally succumbed through his

belief in his great financial ability, and appropriated securities right
and left. This likewise was written a short while before his dealings
were uncovered. Rather a nervous T, is it not? Fortunately he had

No. 15

lenient associates. The last word heard of him was that he was operat-
ing tout for a bucket shop in one of our large Western cities.

At this point it is evident that No. 16 is a weak member, inefficient
through a lack of stable character. And being endowed with this, if
conditions were favorable he would "crook" in a petty fashion. The
cowardly pilferer who runs to cover, usually attempting to "pass the

No. 16

buck" to one of his companions or subordinates. The word "inst"
at this writing shows his uncertain and worried state of mind. Among
special types who graft in politics, who collect commissions on the side,
will be found numerous illustrations resembling, wholly or in part, his
writing.

In like manner, the muddy, vulgar aspect revealed by No. 17 places
this writer in high regard among thugs, gangsters and others using

brutal methods to get their pelf and swag. You can be assured from this grossness and the other thief-signs that this person will be an adept

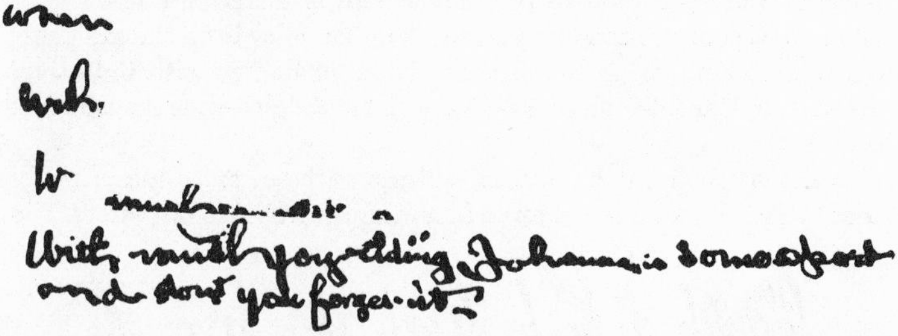

[handwritten specimen]

No. 17

—the same as others writing in a similar style—in rolling pills, dispensing "coke," forcibly extorting blackmail from both women and men. Should your acquaintance extend to the gangster type, I suggest that you take a good look at their script before engaging them for positions as chauffeurs, mechanics or even gardeners.

REVEALS THE COUNTERFEITER

The marked unlikeness of No. 18 to his fellows in shady adventure sets him apart almost in a class by himself. You notice how minutely

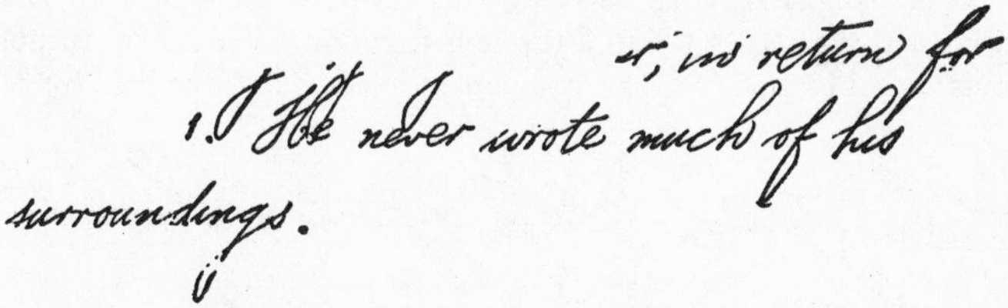

[handwritten specimen]

No. 18

he forms his pen-prints, as though his mind was needlelike in its fashion of applying himself to his job. You can picture him with the blue prints, the metals and dies—a press—turning out with rare skill counterfeit money. His high disproportionate capital "H" shows that he would succumb to the influence of a flattering and cleverer crook. His compression of style means his cupidity is on the rampage, and it is ravenous. In no sense a strong character with initiative! His writing is feeble and of a delicacy resembling the fine instruments he uses.

A deviation from the normal and the paths of rectitude in many cases is due to excessive emotional and uncontrollable outbursts. So

No. 19

No. 19 depicts in his peculiar and rather extraordinary scratches an unbalanced nature ready to take almost any risk in dissipation. Every down stroke is replete with cowardice—moral and physical.

This is the type which readily becomes a victim to the daring criminal, one who would pay any price to escape notoriety or any suspicion of irregular living. Among this class are some women who, fearing an exposé, "give up," through fear and an inability to hold themselves in rein. So the companion piece exhibited in No. 20,

No. 20

manifestly of a distinctly different style, calls out that the individual is one who would use force—a quiet force—to make an emotional and flighty person yield to his demands. He would accomplish what he set out to do, smoothly and with reckless confidence. A mental confidence! He writes with vigor and determination. Money first and always would be his object.

From my experience with these human exhibits and countless others traveling the same way, large or small, proficient or mere trailers in the wake of crime, I find that no one class of society is exempt from furnishing its quota. In fact, luxurious surroundings, indulgent parents and friends and too liberal allowances of money help to intensify into action traits which otherwise would be held in abeyance.

It has been asked what percentage of human beings possess crooked traits. From collected data, I regret to say, about 85 per cent. Rather staggering, is it not?

8

CHAPTER IX

CRIMINALITY

In connection with the method of detecting criminals, there are certain types that disclose specific hand-movements which distinguish their unravelling qualifications. To ferret out and apprehend persons who belong to the criminal classes, confers a peculiar ability. Confidence, force, energy, shrewdness, alertness, judgment and resolute purpose are in evidence. Hence, the signs are positive, specific and clear. The writing is firm, steady, sharp, with emphatic strokes and bold t-crossings. Letters are usually pointed at the base lines and at the top, and fairly well-closed. Final letters end abruptly with downward strokes straight below the lines. The lines are well-spaced with good margins. Capitals are large, high, assertive and frequently flourished.

Combine these signs and it is easy to interpret their meaning and value. And in view of this, observe that the individuals who have inscribed their pen-personalities, stand forth in their own especial niche and place in the country.

Washington D. C Apr 13.

My dear Mr General

I have your letter of the 6 -th and was greatly interested in what you are doing and to learn the pleasure of meeting you on my next visit to New York

Yours very truly

Sincerely yours

W. P. Berne

No. 1. A strong mind, will-power, determination, with keen perception and reserved force are shown. Administrative ability is indicated.

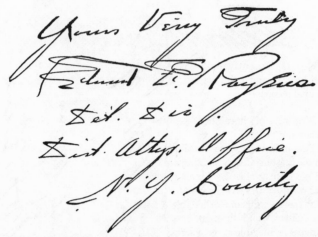

No. 2.   Intelligent, acute, far-sighted, cool and wise.   The skill to plan and execute with a fine sense in arriving at conclusions.

No. 3.   Daring, courageous, resourceful, and wide-awake.   Assertive and self-confident.   Positive type.

No. 4. Executive-manager type who has keen penetration, is level-headed and calm under all emergencies. Master of details of criminal records.

Weakness of character is measured by the absence of moral traits or they are twisted.

The indications are readily disclosed. Thus, dishonesty shows undulating base lines, small letters of even height and size, with a's and o's tightly closed. Finals are cut short. Cunning and ruse are intensified by the writing pointed at the top. M's and n's especially. Theft merely adds one other sign,—hooks at the ends of words.

Gunmen, hold-up men, murderers all exhibit a heavy, coarse, changeable, illegible style of script. Capitals are irregularly made with eccentric flourishes. In most cases, the hand wavers in forming numerous tremors, the indications of the use of morphine, cocaine, heroin and what not. They are known as "dope fiends" or "snow birds."

Crimes are due to lust, passion, lack of money, revenge and hatred.

This criminal directory contains specimens of writing and signatures. Note as follows:

C	stands for	Crook
E	"	"	Embezzler
F	"	"	Forger
H	"	"	Hold-up man, robber
M	"	"	Murderer, gunman
T	"	"	Thief, pickpocket

there ought to be a law

No. 1. T. Thief, pickpocket.

I left just you leave forwarding

No. 2.　E. Embezzler.

described it, indig

No. 3.　C. Crook.

to the act of th

No. 4.　C. Crook and white slaver.

and will probably by 7.

No. 5.　C. Crook.

made for the proposed legislation

No. 6.　C. Crook.

No. 7.   Forger.

No. 8.   Forger.

No. 9.   Hold-up man and robber.

No. 10.   Hold-up man and robber.

No. 11.   Hold-up man and robber.

No. 12.   Hold-up man and robber.

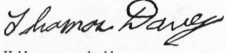

No. 13. Hold-up man and robber.

No. 14. Murderer.

No. 15. Murderer.

No. 16. Murderer.　　　　No. 17. Murderer.

No. 18. Murderer, gunman.　　　　No. 19. Murderer, gunman.

No. 20. Murderer, gunman.　　　　No. 21. Murderer, gunman.

CHAPTER X

SCIENCE

SCIENCE in the realm of hand-movements in writing presents a series of strokes which are plain. In nearly every instance, the usual style is fixed, while the connections are original, and the small letters are low, pointed at the top, needle-like. Individual letters often formed similar to figures or printed, again like musical notes. There are angles more than curves, a prominent feature. It requires analytical skill to differentiate the types of minds which lean toward one phase of science or another. Still, the hall-marks cover the fields of science, research work, medicine, surgery, engineering, or chemistry, or what not.

No. 1. Mineralist.

No. 2. Anthropologist—Signature and circles show uncommunicativeness.

[handwriting sample]

No. 3.   Ethnologist.

[handwriting sample]

No. 4.   Mechanical Engineer.

[handwriting sample]

No. 5.   Scientific Antiquary.

[handwriting sample]

No. 6.   Research in Architecture—Signature denotes eccentricity.

[handwriting sample]

No. 7.   Electrical mechanic.

Dear Mr. French:

I am looking forward with interest to your coming book on "The Psychology of Handwriting". The subject interests me. —Wm H Meadowcroft

No. 8.   Expert in Electricity.

$(as P_2O_5)$, soluble in an artificial

No. 9.   Chemist Specialist.

No. 10.   Technical Engineer.

B. T. B. Hyde

No. 11.   Explorator type, Archæologist.

[signature]

No. 12.   Surgery, Specialist.

[signature]

No. 13.   Surgery, Specialist.

[signature]

No. 14.   Surgery, Specialist.

CHAPTER XI

EDITORIAL AND LITERARY STYLE

EDITORS are numerous, but in one aspect, they all display an appearance which is characteristic to one degree. Each individual has his own style, his specialized capitals, but the lines are well-spaced both above and below, letters low or very low and sharpened at the top. Where the writing is partially rounded with some letters disconnected, then a keen value of new ideas and fresh conceptions is denoted. So, those who act in this capacity are apt to take the initiative in following their judgment. The individuals who are here exhibited will be both efficient and productive in their capabilities. The series are so numbered that the reader is enabled to gauge the qualities of the writers by following the directions specified.

No. 1. Finely poised, keen, positive.

An obstacle is simply a difficulty to overcome.

Edward W. Bok

April 1922

No. 2.   Mental force and energy.   Imagination.

No. 3.   Creative ability, shrewd, energetic.

No. 4.   Large conceptions, managerial ability.

No. 5.   Alert, intellectual virility.

No. 6.   Literary insight, concentration.

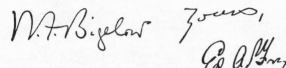 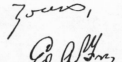

| No. 7. Clear thinker, calm, decisive in opinions. | No. 8. Intellectual honesty, wide view-point. |

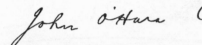

No. 9. Analytical mind, cautious, virile principles.

No. 10. Competent, resourceful, sharp perception.

No. 11. Versatile, big conceptions, foresight.

| No. 12. Mental alertness, executive ability. | No. 13. Artistic, imaginative, versatile. |

No. 14.   Wide vision, broadmindedness, executive sense.

No. 15.   Shrewd, quick active brain, broad, positive.

No. 16.   Continuity and intense application of ideas.

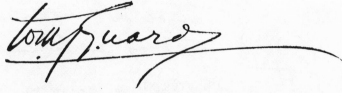

No. 17.   Vivid imagination, creative faculty.

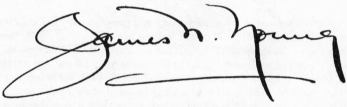

No. 18.   Acumen, keen vision, original ideas.

No. 19.   Analytical, critical, sure, reserve force.

CHAPTER XII

SENSUOUSNESS is the quality every one possesses who has artistic appreciation and taste. The chief features are to be noted. First, the shading of the down and cross strokes are frequently pronounced, revealing an intense love of beauty in all of its forms. Second, the script is unique, original; connections are well-made, lines not interfering with another, while breaks take place between some of the letters. The upper portion of the long letters extend well above the lines. Generally the capitals are artistically formed, curved, printed or oddly constructed. A distinctive type is that of the small "d" where the final backward stroke curls to the left above the stem of the letter. Often the Greek "e" appears. The rounded form of "w" and "n" shows talent for writing verse.

Now the members of the group here exhibited, have all the hallmarks which display literary gifts in one direction or another.

No. 1.

No. 2.

130

Yours Sincerely

Frances Hodgson Burnett

No. 3.

Yours Truly,

Rex Beach

No. 4.

Mary Roberts Rinehart

No. 5.

have gone so far as to call it an unnatural hand.

Yours Sincerely

To William Leslie French, Esq.   Irvin S. Cobb.

No. 6.

No. 7.

No. 8.

No. 9.

No. 10.

No. 11.

No. 12.

I have to doubt that my handwriting
shows I have an unbalanced mind
on the stomach and am lazy, fond of fishing
and a democrat, but you can use it in a
book if you wish.

With best wishes
Ellen Parker Butler

No. 13.

James Oliver Curwood.

No. 14.

Basil King

No. 15.

Edward Fredric Benson

No. 16.

Arthur Conan Doyle   *H. G. Wells*

No. 17.   No. 18.

H. Rider Haggard

No. 19.

J. M. Barrie

No. 20.

Joseph Conrad.

No. 21.

W. J. Locke

No. 22.

Eden Phillpotts

No. 23.

Gabriele d'Annunzio
Dal Benàco, 1921.

No. 24.

CHAPTER XIII

ART, MUSIC AND THE DRAMA

As we approach the realm of art, where color, form, music, and the drama hold sway, the evidences in any of these classes are distinct. They differ largely in the manner in which the shading of the strokes is made and the fashion of forming the capitals. Generally speaking, the heavier the shading of the down strokes the greater the appeal to the sensuous side of existence, while the lightness or thickness of the cross strokes denotes the degree of susceptibility to everything that appeals to the senses of sight and hearing. Hence, individuals who are especially responsive to beauty and art are inclined to shade their cross strokes. The greater the sensitiveness, the lighter these will be. By observing, then, the varied forms the capitals exhibit and the method of shading, it is possible to learn in what line of artistic endeavor a person is liable to show talent.

When genius and gifts for painting or sculpture are given, the penformations are plainly indicated, as follows:

The script is harmonious, often bizarre or original, the down strokes heavy or shaded, with capitals graceful and artistic. Sometimes, these are similar to printed designs. By an examination it is possible to determine these pen-personalities who are "hung" for selection according to their genius.

In order to show how a man has a writing marked with spiritual strength, he also reveals that he was well-known as a landscape artist and particularly deft at water-color design. Here his wide spacings between words and letters denote his single-minded and liberal attitude toward everybody, despite their failings. It caused him to forgive and forget, and in the exhibition of this spirit to be generous almost before he was just to himself. His vertical style signifies that his mind and heart

Compelled to hard
the.support of the

No. 1.

are equally balanced, which is modified in this particular by the lightness of the down and cross strokes—symbolizing purity and great spirituality. It increases his affection towards his fellowmen. In both phases, both intellectual powers and application are utilized for his art, as his connecting strokes, height of his small, rather low letters, with large, looped l's in combination denote. His style is in equipoise of character and ability.

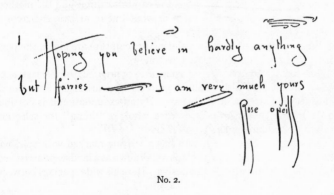

No. 2.

poor old moth eaten school teacher Drop me a line — Very sincerely J Francis Murphy

No. 3.

No. 4.

Always sincerely yrs Henrietta Cholmeley Jones

No. 5.

No. 6.

[signature]

No. 7.

[signature]

No. 8.

[signature]

No. 9.

Jan 8 '20

A painter copies nature
An artist idealizes + creates

C. Becker

No. 10.

In "The
Psychology of Handwriting"
you are indeed treating upon
a most interesting subject
and I wish you and your
book every success
Sincerely yours,
Orland Campbell.

No. 11.

No. 12.

The leading signs which show a talent for sculpture are pen-forms uniform, more or less original, small letters are comparatively low, with down and cross strokes shaded.

No. 13.

No. 14.

No. 15.

Music is the one art that appeals to the ear, both voice and instrumental. It appeals to the spirit, to the mind and the soul. And we feel its effects without any special effort. So, with the sense of tune and rhythm, there is the rounding sweep at the bottom of the letters that reflects a keen ear for melody, and the shading,—musical sensuousness. The capitals are graceful, curved, and strongly and artistically shaped. Melodious expression produces a gliding motion, with cross strokes shaded. Harmony and technique will present sharpened forms at the top in addition. The talent will appear where the artist shows also force, perseverance and will-power. The hand-movements are firm and vital.

These few represent musical talent and even genius.

"One who has learned
an art in his youth
can never be wholly
unhappy"

Jeanne Gordon

No. 16.

yours Truly

Nelle Handell

No. 17.

affettuosi saluti e credimi tuo
affmo
Enrico Caruso

No. 18.

To William Leslie French
Wishing a big Success
to your new book the:
Psychology of handwriting

Claudia Muzio

No. 19.

And in like manner, the signs of dramatic talent are clearly indicated. The predominant features are the size, form and shape of the capitals. Large curves are numerous, especially. Observe that the connections are free and extensive. The script is flowing, with universal use of cross and down strokes which are shaded, showing the responsiveness to color, light, music and beauty. There is an irregular wavy movement of the base lines, sometimes sweeping in an arc formation. The combination of capitals together with the undulation of the lines represent the qualities which individuals possess, and whom the drama as a profession calls,—those whose mental propensities cry aloud impersonation, pride, independence, love of approbation, self-esteem and the desire to succeed. As we regard these written personalities, it is easy to see why they are individual.

No. 20.

No. 21.

No. 22.

"There's no such thing as
'mascots' man's got to
be his own 'mascot.'"

From
"Bunker Bean".

Very sincerely,

Taylor Holmes

No. 23.

With pleasure!
Faithfully
Florence Reed

No. 24.

My dear Mrs French

~~Don't~~ be too hard

on me. I'm a rather penman

and know it

       Best wishes

       Donald Brian

No. 25.

Sincerely Yours

Allen Curtis Jenkins

No. 26.

Minnie Dupree

No. 27.

With all best wishes   *Sincerely yours*
Bruce McRae

No. 28.

are welcome to it. Its not teeming with grace & elegance, is it?

Yours
DeWolf Hopper

No. 29.

Mary Shaw.

No. 30.

Each time I make someone laugh, in
this world, where there is so much sorrow & care,
I feel that—I have accomplished something
worthwhile

Joseph Cawthorn

No. 31.

Yours Sincerely,

Otto Kruger

No. 32.

*make believe world
of the Theatre.*

*sincerely yours
Ernest Truex*

No. 33.

Marjorie Rambeau

No. 34.

[Handwriting sample]

No. 35.

CHAPTER XIV

THEY present their strength, courage, mental powers, capacities and abilities, as are revealed in their pen-signs. As self-evident the types and styles are symbolical of American citizenship in the same fashion as the script written by men.

Greetings and good wishes.

Florence Kling Harding.

No. 1. Genial, frank, straight-forward, her nature is hospitable. She understands her own mind and has the desire to express her ideas. Positive but enthusiastic.

Woman Suffrage is bound to come

Mary Garrett Hay.

No. 2. Firm, strong, well-balanced, the writer has a keen intellect. Steady purposes and motives. Logical, calm and collected. Her executive ability is clearly shown.

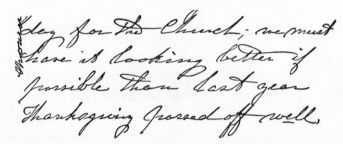

No. 3.   This gentlewoman is high spirited, loyal to friends and foes alike, warm-hearted and generous.   An enormous energy actuating her high beliefs and standards.   Motherly type.

No. 4.   Forceful, active, holding her convictions rigidly, she abides by her ideas.   Tenacious of purpose, she also has executive insight. Talks enthusiastically to the point.

No. 5.   The writer is endowed with a keen analytical mind, with purposeful actions.   Works rapidly, conscientious but impulsive.   Has managerial capacity.

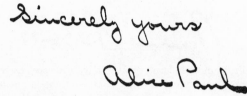

No. 6.   Full of life and vitality, this writer is positive, sure and full
of buoyancy.   She does not know when she is worsted.   Her beliefs and
ideas are always teeming.   Honest.

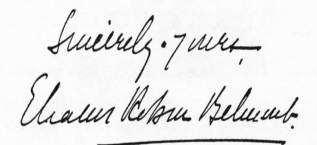

No. 7.   A woman who has a clear intelligence, critical and well-
poised and harmonious in her relationships.   Has a capacity for directing
affairs, but her ideas are practical and sympathetic.

No. 8.   A strong, decided, far-sighted nature, with a vigorous mind
is shown by this writer.   Dominated by her beliefs and conceptions,
she will use them definitely.   High-minded, is her main trait.

No. 9.   Pride, independence, great vitality, intensity are reinforced by a lively imagination and courage.   She is idealistic but has great common sense.   She is energetic, plus!

No. 10.   A dominant personality, with a quick, logical mind, intelligence and great activity.   Original in her views and stands pat under all circumstances, she believes that she is right.   The promoter type.

No. 11.   Poised, active, a strong will and determination are indicated.   Her mind is keen, analytical, and capable of great work. Has executive power, with a mastery of details.   A practical common sense always revealed.

My Slogan is Temperance, but not Prohibition Elsie

Elisabeth Marbury

No. 12. For quick decisive action, will power, self-confidence, this writer is a definite force. Her mental faculties are sharpened by her personality. Her acumen is self-evident. Both executive and sales ability are pronounced.

CHAPTER XV

For several years Mr. French has been engaged in a comparison of the handwriting of men and women. In this chapter he gives a brief statement of his conclusions.

WOMAN is no longer the eternal paradox. Her evolution into the ranks of the procession displaying the world's varied achievements has not been sudden, but dynamically she has entered the lists, a strong and competent competitor of man.

In the realms of art, music, literature and the drama she has penetrated, talented, effective, and a producer. No phase of commercial, religious or even political life but feels the impetus of her personality which, so far as results are concerned, is acknowledged, grudgingly perhaps by some, to be steadily approaching the results produced by man. The eternal feminine, without the loss or charm of sex, is gradually being translated into the positive, vitalizing energy of accomplishment.

There is a scientific reason for all this.

Handwriting is a physical gesture of the mind, no matter what the sex may be. This is due to the close relationship between the brain, nerves and the hand. The "punch" exhibited in the strokes of pen or pencil is the "punch" of personality. This is why one frequently hears, "His writing resembles a person whom I know." Talents and special gifts can be traced out. We all pigeon-hole our acquaintances by their facial expression, gestures or words, though all of these may lie. We can never be sure. The writing gestures are permanent records, because they do not actually change.

I purpose showing that the qualities resident in men are also the

endowment of women—"line upon line"—"here a little, there a little"
—irrespective of what some psychologists and neurologists may say;
and sometimes they say some very curious things.

From the comparison of illustrations to follow, the reader will be
able to see that sex, pure and simple, does not necessarily appear in
handwriting; for both sexes have to a greater or less degree the three
main characteristics: will, judgment or logic, and passion.

At the outset, to render a correct decision concerning the complete
mental and physical equipment of any individual from script, a portion
of the writing and the signature are necessary, as they supplement each
other. What is found in the one is sometimes and frequently absent
in the other. The signature is the keystone completing the human
architectural product.

Glance at Nos. 1 and 2 and you will note a like force, power and
energy. The flowing rapid style, with uniformly firm pressure through-

No. 1.

No. 2.

out, decisive t crossings and well-made connections of words and
letters, show that each individual has will-power, decision, and the ability to reason logically. The parts of the pen-forms balance indicating

equipoise.   Marked continuity of thought, analysis and concentration
appear in the linking together of letters which are low as compared with
the capitals.   Both individuals sharpen their small letters at the top,
signifying great resisting power.   Both are dynamic in achievement.

There is a saying that "the bigger the individual the more striking
the script."   No. 3, by the vigorous, fleet, energetic style, large

No. 3.

capitals, and minutely concentrated small letters, with the extensions
below the line of the long letters, pointed, as in y—gives the writer the
ability to plan and execute, gives initiative, analysis and synthesis.
The steady even writing shows mental balance and clean cut purpose.

No. 4 is markedly different in pressure, the ink being differently
distributed, and one or two minor signs of this appearing.   Yet the

No. 4

same general hall-marks appear.   The running dash and swing exhibit
energy, while the connecting strokes and sharp form throughout reveal
a live mind.   Both of these writers are positive people.

No. 5.

No. 5 is a bit of the handwriting of John Purroy Mitchel. He forces his personality to the front; for his strong, positive, strung-together signature is as determined as his t crossings. He has power of application, and his reasoning faculties are always on the alert. Courage and daring are found in the pressure. If you will take the trouble to examine the writing of many a forceful productive woman, you will find similar signs.

No. 6.

No. 6 does not seem to present the same value, at first sight. But the sharp bold script and high-flung t crossings denote the same general characteristics.

The two styles of script in Nos. 7 and 8 seem strikingly dissimilar. Still, the mental traits revealed are similar. The woman is gov-

No. 7.

erned to a large extent by her affections—she writes at a slant of 45 degrees. The slope of 8 betrays coolness, caution, deliberation. Yet apart from the emotional side, both are endowed with the same amount of intelligence and capabilities. The woman's writing is light, but uniform in pressure. The well-formed connections and forceful t bars show that she has the courage of her opinions. High standards with good judgment appear in the exact even spacing and slant to the right.

No. 8.

She formulates her opinions for herself, and would not need any coaching if permitted to vote. The man pounds the page because he is the type who means business. The blunt formation of the down strokes denotes obstinacy and tenacity. His judgment is good. He knows because he thinks carefully before he acts; he hauls his words together evenly. He would be suspicious of any radical or new movement. Another who writes similarly recently said: "Women are butting in most indecently. I'll be married in spite of myself."

That women possess talent for music, art and the drama, equal to that of men, is clearly shown in Nos. 9 and 10. Note in each case

No. 9.

the original curves, the rhythmic swing of the strokes at the bottom of words, the signs of melody and harmony. The shading of all strokes

is distinctive—denoting the appeal which art in all of its forms makes
to them. The high curved capitals reflect temperament, intense and
responsive. These capitals are found throughout "the profession"

No. 10.

with the undulating base line. The upward swing to the right, excellent
joining of strokes, reflect intelligences which are dominated by ambition
and the desire to achieve in a large way. Although No. 11 is distinc-

No. 11.

tively different in general style, you will see how forcefully the writer expresses personality. She joins the words and letters together—careful
thinking and discretion. She deliberates before expressing her opinion.
Her writing is unimpassioned, showing that emotionality is not her
guide. It is upright. Her m's and n's pointed at the top, reveal a keen
critical faculty.

The literary "d"—found frequently in the handwriting of authors
—appears! She could produce, if she chose, but not necessarily in an
imaginative way. Her strokes above the line, the long letters—are not
looped or very large. Her function would be to choose, to select with
good judgment. No. 12 has the same elements but distributed in

another way. The steady, even, vertical script denotes that the writer would exercise discretion, caution and care. He has the intellect to

No. 12.

produce. Imaginative work, pure and simple, is his metier. His mind in operation works with intense application.

Where you find high capitals, heavy, pronounced shading combined with very orderly writing, you may be sure that the individual is opinionated, conceited and believes in "the grand old party" in politics, whatever that may be. Such a writer would be intolerant of a woman being anything except a domestic animal. The simple, unassuming style of writing means that the writer would not have great aggressiveness or push. Blunt downward strokes and connections well made indicate that the writer would think and not actually be swayed against his or her will. Slant shows a devotion to ideals, a normal thinking apparatus, and stubborn adherence to principles. In a woman this is the type who would seize the opportunity to vote to benefit her home and children, sacrificing everything to that end. Such a woman when she reached the polls would not trade her simple and honest ambition for any price. There are thousands of both men and women who write in this plain and simple manner. Positive and virile connecting strokes, strong original capitals, and heavy application of ink, signify self-assurance, initiative, individual and commanding force, while small letters written large, coupled with high extensions above the lines, show expansive conceptions with a power to put them into effect, physical equipoise and marked intelligence. Even base lines indicate honesty of purpose.

Sharp, decided holograph, a minute concentrated method of making small letters pointed at the bottom and top, perfect connections, all denote acute penetration, a keen analytical sense, observation even to inquisitiveness, logic and reason. A virile imagination is shown by high loopings of h and l. Words uniformly heavy and connected indicate determination and tenacity. Capitals remarkably curved, expressive, original, are signs of fleet mental action. A flamboyant imagination is shown by a rounded shape of letters above the line. An erratic form, plus a dominant pressure of all down strokes reveals a responsiveness to rhythm and melody.

Even in this brief survey, with but a very limited number of specimens possible for interpretation, there is abundant evidence that the characteristics and intellectual equipment of women, their force and efficiency, are on a par with those of men. They are taking places in the world's activities not because they are women, necessarily, but because, given the opportunity, they have been equipped to improve it.

It is to be thoughtfully considered that of the thousands of writings which have passed under my observation, 15,000 or more, the sign of protection, of devotion to an ideal and the tendency for work for the common good, appear. I wish I could say the same as regards my own sex. The writing of ninety per cent. of women gives evidence of these tendencies.

The signs are: The inclination to write vertically, or to the right; wide spacings between words and letters and a backward stroke to left, as in the y, turning to the left. All these denote a lack of selfishness.

That handwriting should reveal the signs of the times, the undercurrent of opinion, is not so remarkable as we think. It reveals, in countless examples, that equality of the sexes is not a vagary, a false claim; and what these few examples of handwriting reveals is proven by what women are achieving daily in the most widely varied fields of human endeavors.

CHAPTER XVI

THE MARRIAGE RELATIONSHIP

THE Gretna Green where character and temperament are perfectly wedded together, is the script of the individual, because it is the outward symbol of the mind's action through the nerve connection with its agent, the hand. While much can be told from gesture, gait and facial expression, they are only partially equipped guides to a person's mental and physical trend. The involuntary and voluntary penstrokes are permanent signs which can easily be interpreted by comparison and analysis of the slant of the writing, sweep of the words, letter formations and shading of strokes.

Over a century ago it was discovered that special types of handwriting were inscribed by individuals possessing like traits and characteristics. Where, say, fifty of a certain class wrote alike, it was observed that the fifty-first making pen-forms similarly, was a reproduction of the others. By pursuing this method still further, the finest shades of character, temperament and disposition were reached. In fact, it has been demonstrated a host of times that special styles of handwriting will indicate gifts and talents for one line of work or another.

At the outset it will be well to inform the reader that in France and Germany for a century or more, and latterly in England, this science of handwriting has been studied and practised. Its value in criminal cases has been recognized by the courts, apart from the work of handwriting experts; and in commercial circles, graphologists have been employed as interpreters of script in situations where honesty, integrity, accuracy and faithfulness are the prime requisites. Graphology has been defined as the insurance of labor, the risk being that of character. The twin forces determining the premium are personality and pen.

Among the leading authorities are the German poet Goethe and the French author l'abbé Michon. In their native tongues they taught and made clear the practical utility of graphology in revealing to men their fellowmen. And in both Germany and France illustrated journals are published devoted entirely to all phases of this subject. Also, it is of more than passing interest that in recent times in the famous "Bordereau" relative to the Dreyfus case, the decisions of the graphologists were of eminent assistance in proving his innocence, in marked contrast to the handwriting experts. This fact, however, has not generally been commented upon.

Now, a true friend or helpmeet is the best medium of exchange both in periods of happiness as well as stress, and in order to insure permanent satisfaction and enjoyment from the companionship of others, whether friend or lover, husband or wife, a trustworthy guide to this end will be hailed with interest.

The writer has found in numerous script specimens coming under his observation for analysis, that much of the trouble which has resulted from persons being lawfully, but unfortunately, allied by marriage, was due to the fact that the attraction drawing them together had no stability other than attraction. Their characters were sealed volumes to each other. Had each one's writing been examined expertly, it might have proved a deterrent against future disaster. And be it said, that the advantage of using this method in contrast to others, is obvious. All that is necessary is a small sample with or without signature. No further data is required. Only the script. The strokes tell the story. That this is so, anyone can easily verify by an examination of any two specimens written by the same person at different times. If the individual is influenced by some great emotion, especially sorrow or trouble, the caligraphy will alter, showing a signal departure from the normal, the most marked sign being, that the final words of lines to the right have a tendency to slope downward.

Again, today, owing to the new conditions created by the higher education of women, it is much more difficult to determine sex from script. Every profession and line of work are affected by their endeavors and influence, and in consequence, the leading traits of will power, judgment and self-confidence appear in their strokes, to a far greater degree than heretofore.

Turn now to that phase of graphology which naturally makes its appeal to every human being, because it furnishes data which help toward the realization of happiness. Each person looks forward to the time when he or she shall find a true helpmeet—and in every sense of the word—a friend. In general, the leading characteristics which we try to discover in those for whom we entertain affection, are honesty, sincerity, steadfastness, loyalty and love. These traits are shown for the most part by handwriting sloping to the right or somewhat vertical words clearly written, with the lines straight.

By glancing at Nos. 1 and 2 (above) you will find the script of two individuals who are as perfect a complement of each other as could be found. The holograph of each slants perceptibly to the right, indicating deep abiding love and the tendency to idolize each other. No. 1, the man, has a strong will and determination, shown by the even pressure and the crossings. This combined with the slope gives steadfastness and tenderness. The spaces between words, letters, and lines with the outward strokes in some of the final letters formed as in "*read*," betray generosity and sympathy. His attitude, or any one writing in this fashion, is one that would be ideal as a lover, husband or friend. Specimen No. 2, the woman, sloping at even a greater angle in a like direction, denotes even a greater amount of sentiment. The spacings are the same, but her script runs uphill a trifle more than his, indicating hopefulness and courage. The trait of generous feeling is paramount to everything else.

Her sensitiveness—the delicate strokes—her intuition—the breaks between the letters as in "i s"—endow her with a special sense which enables her to feel the mental condition of her consort and thus avoid friction. There are other minor traits which have no bearing at this

If you can read this you are perfectly welcome—
This is not a business Transaction. Yours very Truly

(Specimen No. 1)

Type of man who would make an ideal lover or husband (No. I)

Tommy through the Lakes Country is beyond description. Do wish you were journeying with us to help us eat the Black Bass and to help in the cooking thereof—

Type of woman who would make an ideal wife (No. 2)

(Specimen No. 2)

point.   This couple have enjoyed a tender relationship for many years. Where the writing is upright, in either sex, the other formations being similar, the individual, would be less demonstrative, especially if the final letters end abruptly.

Should, by an haphazard of misfortune, the writers of Nos. 3, a man, and 4 a woman, or any who write like them, ever marry, or even contemplate it, they would fight like Kilkenny cats on the back fence.

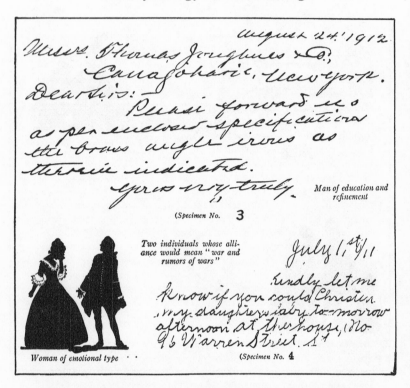

(Specimen No. **3**

Man of education and
refinement

Two individuals whose alliance would mean "war and
rumors of wars"

Woman of emotional type

(Specimen No. **4**

These handwritings are as absolutely mismated as the individuals
would be. Both have the slant to the right. But—alas! though this
does denote broadly affection, so many other modifications appear,
that it is lost in the fog of clashing traits on both sides. The man is
naturally ambitious, straightforward and honest, shown by regular
even pressure, straight lines and upward movement. Order and system
are his strong points. He is immaculate in his dress, but he is as ob-

stinate as a mule, with a desire to boss. This is indicated by the blunt ending of some of the strokes and the t crossings. The lack of sympathy appears in the last stroke of final letters, while the large, rounded capitals show conceit. His general style indicates refinement and education.

Now if this individual *should* marry the writer of No. 4,—immediately there would be "wars and rumors of wars," as his whole mental trend and habits of life would be different from hers, even though she might be very attractive on the physical plane. Observe the halting, simple style without any marked character to it! Affection is there—the slant shows that. Her will-power is almost negative, as the uneven pressure and t-bars indicate. It is not her fault that her sympathy would bubble over at every funeral she could attend. She would incline to tears readily, enjoy being delightfully miserable, which would naturally grate upon any man with a disposition like her husband's. The small o's being open at the top give her a desire to talk unnecessarily at all times. Household gods and goods she worships. But her sense of fitness would cause her to crochet tidies and cultivate wax flowers under a glass. A good salesman could sell her crayon pictures of her entire family, later to be hung with a background of wall paper of red roses and purple lilies. All this is betrayed by her general style. Her sense of order is lacking. Yet she would scrub hard. Emotionally strong—shading of letters and slope of writing—her devotion would be explosive, and her temper, as typified by the cross strokes, very fitful. Despite whatever physical beauty either of these, or any like them, might possess, their pen formations no more harmonize than in actual life their alliance would be blessed by congeniality.

Now, should a woman whose script resembles that of No. 5 think of joining forces with a man who writes a hand like No. 6 it would be well for her to pause and consider! The same holds good as regards the man. Both would have set ideals with much sentiment. The slope again. In each, the pressure is alike, revealing force and will-power. The larger style and shape of the letters in the woman's hand show a tendency to rush things. Her capitals denote self-assurance

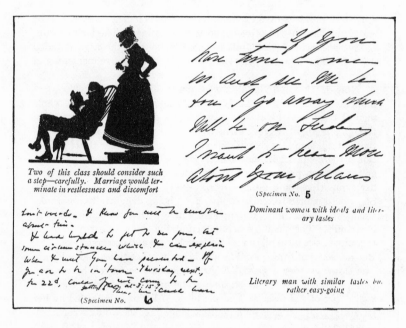

Two of this class should consider such a step—carefully. Marriage would terminate in restlessness and discomfort

(Specimen No. **5**)

Dominant woman with ideals and literary tastes

(Specimen No. **6**)

Literary man with similar tastes but rather easy-going

and a sense of importance, while the open a's and g's indicate that she would dominate in the expression of her opinions. The t crossing and blunt final letters signify her ruling capacity, despite the fact that she would enjoy a discussion of literature and art. Her energy is pervasive.

With the man's script you find a tremendous power of concentration. This is indicated by the small writing. The even pressure throughout, combined with wide spaces, betrays steadiness, a generous attitude, while the slope to the right without cross-bars, reveals a sentiment which makes for peace and calmness. The lack of harmony between these two would exist from the fact that her desire to forge ahead, putting her ideas into action, would clash with this peaceable disposition.   There are no bold, arrogant cross-bars in his script.   Any two of this class would get along provided each followed independently individual tastes and ambitions.   They should agree to disagree comfortably.

These two types would be very un-comfortable!   They might marry

*no moral principle.
Our handwriting is a
thing imperishable.
By it "the living epistle
is not known and heard
of all men, but known
and read."*

(Specimen No. 7

Peace-loving, peace-cultivating man

*but in order to explain clearly the idealism
of our movement, the hopes and aspirations of
its leaders, and how equal suffrage works
out where it is being tried: There exists a*

(Specimen No.   8

Woman of too much force

The scripts Nos. 7 and 8 above have common aims, denoted by the clear, steady, even strokes, animated by honesty and sincerity, as the straight lines and even height of small letters show; still an alliance of any two such persons would be marred by mental conflict and reservations.   The easy, flowing style and delicate writing of the man is a positive sign of a genial, quiet disposition.   He is never in a flurry.

The woman has too much force. Her ambition and determination, as per her heavy writing, down strokes and t crossings, would carry him into an atmosphere of physical discomfort and mental unrest. They would not of necessity clash madly. Merely the woman is too strong, and her almost vertical hand shows that her mind dominates her feelings and affections. Vice versa as regards the man.

Now in the types shown by Nos. 9 and 10, although the script of each is very dissimilar on sight, there are many points in common.

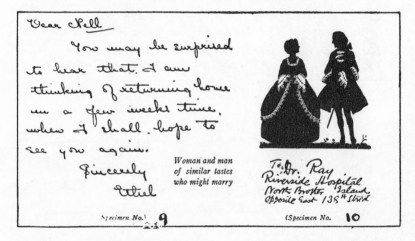

Woman and man
of similar tastes
who might marry

Specimen No. 9

(Specimen No. 10

The woman, No. 9, writes a hand which though vertical, betraying coldness and reserve, yet the shaded, uneven down strokes make her sensuous and responsive to beauty in all of its forms. The rounded formation of her small letters at the bottom reveals musical talent. This corresponds with all that appears in her side companion, No. 10, even though the slant is different. There would be a distinct harmony in their point of view, but of these two, or any like them, the preponderance of affection would be with the man. Not much emotion, however, would be betrayed on either side. Such types can meet on the common ground of similarity of tastes and moderate friendship.

Type of script revealing dishonesty and lying. A man (No. 11

Style of writing which shows nervous tension and tendency to exaggerate. A woman (No 12

(Specimen No. 11

(Specimen No. 12

Script No. 11 (above), reveals a type of man of whom to beware, apart from any personality or power of attraction he may have. He is unbridled in his desires—note the heavy, vile, down strokes! The wavy base lines being very much in evidence, with the closed o's, signify that he is a liar and thoroughly dishonest. The erratic formation of his connected letters gives a strong personality. Anyone writing in this way should be avoided. Also, generally speaking, with any man or woman whose writing flows in this undulating fashion, whether of this script type or not, the tendency to deceit is paramount. Of course, other signs might modify this tendency, such as will power, shown by strong pressure throughout.

In No. 12, a woman (above), are similar conditions. In her case the nervous, erratic method of forming her pen pictures, the long letters of one line extending into that below, is indicative of a mental twist. She would believe absolutely in the images created by her imagination. High, nervous tension is denoted by the dotting of her i's and punctuation.

As you examine No. 13, you would hardly credit brutality to such a script. Yet it is so. The individual's tastes and actions are of the most inferior brand. His capital-letter-formations show extreme vulgarity and egotism, intensified by the heavy strokes contrasted with light. His writing is sharp on top, the sign of mental alertness. This combined with the small letters being very close together, signifies meanness and selfishness. When a man like this one spends money it is for attaining ignoble ends. His physical prowess is shown by the long, down stroke below the line in "*Yours.*" Cunning is denoted by the sharp small letters. Because of this he would win over an adversary. In fact, as a prize fighter and politician he has been successful. Most men following this "profession" have these script forms in one combination or another. The style often differs, though the analytical results are the same.

As a climax in exhibits, No. 14 shows a personality, eccentric, brilliant, but from the standpoint of marriage, an utter failure. The capitals shout inordinate conceit, sensitiveness and false pride. The unexpected, extraordinary curves and extra twists furnish an unbounded imagination. The writing waves—a liar! Extravagance throws its head plainly above the horizon, as the spacing shows. In this instance, as in all like his, the shading of the down strokes and cross

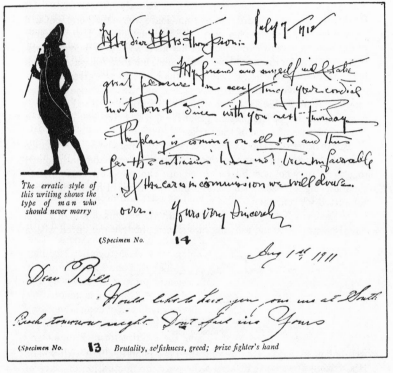

The erratic style of this writing shows the type of man who should never marry

(Specimen No. 14)

(Specimen No. 13) Brutality, selfishness, greed; prize fighter's hand

bars indicate utter self-indulgence. Should such a man marry he would soon break away, leaving sorrow in his wake. Whenever such erratic signs appear the individual, man or woman, is oscillating, changeable, and literally changes with the moon. Usually, however, possessing charm and a striking personality!

It has been said that a boy's will is the wind's will, and it is on record that many a man is like the boy when brought face to face with

12

marriage. His ideal is subject to change. But a woman's will is most frequently directed toward finding some mate whose temperament will harmonize and complete her own.   Wisely enough, she is more likely to desire some definite knowledge of her lover's traits and characteris-tics than he. Her interest alone would cause her to investigate, though her faith in him were great, before her final consent was given.

Manners have changed with the times, and the avoidance of matri-mony by many is due to the scepticism and wisdom acquired by young men and women of the present generation, who hold aloof because of the experiences of some of their friends.

But in order that those who are thus inclined may have a fair chance from the start, and that the words, "Those whom God hath joined together," may not possibly be turned into a hollow sham and reproach, the following additional suggestions and specimens of handwriting are submitted for reflection.

A glance at No. 15 reveals the characteristic signs of a man whose moral nature is strong, showing him sincere, honest and gifted with a

No. 15.   Strong moral nature, sincere, honest, well-
balanced mind

well-balanced mind. He is resolute and fair in his dealings with others. His writing flows straight across the page, no fluctuation or wave of the lines, and his pressure is uniform, while he crosses his t's with decision. Candor is shown in a few of his a's and o's being open.   The angle of his script, nearly forty-five degrees, indicates that his affections are deep-seated, while generosity of feeling and act appear in the final strokes of the letters. These signs indicate that he would sacrifice himself for wife and children, while peace and happiness would be the lot of his side-partner. He is not close in money matters—the wide spacing between words and letters shows this. A woman filled with affection, ambition, hopefulness and sensitive pride could entrust her well-being to such a writer with the assurance that no matter what her foibles might be, they would be sympathetically understood and forgiven in advance.

No. 16 is the writing of a woman who could happily mate with anyone who shows the pen traits of No. 15.

No. 16.   Type of woman who would mate happily
with No. 15

By contrast No. 17 hardly seems, at first sight, to possess all of the same characteristics, so far as disposition and character are concerned. But it is so! The vertical script shows control of the emotions and

No. 17.   Shows control of emotions and feelings

feelings, which in No. 15 is found in the heavier pressure. A like generosity appears in the wide spacings—in this case more pronounced. This is the type whose liberality of thought and sympathy would go out to everyone—to those of his family particularly, and especially his wife.

Whenever men, young or old, throw much force into their strokes, using uniformly heavy pressure, the stems of the long letters extending well below the base line, either rounded or straight, they are endowed with strong physiques, great powers of endurance and clear minds— always, when the strokes of one line do not interfere with the others.

Nos. 18, 19, and 20 are those which give the clues that reflect the ability to stand pat under all conditions or any circumstances. An

No. 18.   Perfect physical and mental health shown in
y's and initials

No. 19.   The same indicated as in No. 18

No. 20.   Small f and g show he is in the same class

alliance with any of these types would give a guarantee that a woman could always feel that her mate would ever be on the hustle to support her faithfully.   All three indicate reliability, affection and decency, though the slope in each is different.   No erratic splashes, no vulgar heavy shading of the downstrokes, no deceptive base lines or wobbling words!

On the other hand, if a man seeks in his wife energy, perseverance, loftiness of purpose and ability to work side by side as a partner, No. 21 possesses all the hall-marks.   The gradual upward slope to the right,

No. 21.   Excellent side partner, ambition and
energy shown

rapid style, steady pressure and even height of small letters are excellent signs. This writer's disposition would cause her to work for harmony and home despite the cost, while her affections are very decided.

No. 22 is the type who reveals a calm, easy-going disposition, for the most part ambitious, amiable, sympathetic and generous. The rounded formation of the letters, upward open curves of finals, wide spaces between words and letters show these qualities. She would

No. 22. Easy-going disposition, sympathetic, generous

sacrifice herself for husband, children and friends, being devoted to everything which pertains to personal improvement, religion and learning. If the t bar were higher, she would be inclined to temper and faultfinding.

The slow swing of the writing in No. 23 with the curved letters, not too heavy pressure, moderate slant and round finals, signifies that this woman would be devoted to the interests of those she loves, not fretful

No. 23. Devotion to those whom she loves

or hysterical, but would be inclined to lean upon the affections of the man she had married. His will would be law. She would regard his

efforts with admiration.   When ill she would be constantly at his side.
She is not one who would interfere in his work.

No. 24 is of like character, only her sensitiveness to criticism, shown
in the backward stroke of the t's, would prevent her from taking a joke,
and she would take seriously any remarks concerning her doing her

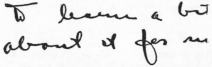

No. 24.   Performs duties seriously, sensitive

duty.   That she would show her feelings very freely is indicated by the
upright style and the abrupt ending of words.   She is less likely than
No. 23 to be demonstrative.

The qualities of brilliancy, dash, enthusiasm, liveliness, tact, emotion, ambition to shine socially, or in any other capacity, appear in
No. 25.   They are indicated by the large, curved capital, by the first

No. 25.   Would shine socially as a social leader

small letters of words being larger at the beginning than at the end, and
by the undulating base line.   The high crossing of the t means the desire
to rule.   These signs give to the man who desires such a companion for
life the right clue.

A tender-hearted, frank and spiritually minded girl or woman,
penning a hand sloping much to the right, light in pressure, a's and o's

being open at the top, with capital "M" or "W" high— No. 26 is a
good illustration—setting her affection upon a man who writes like

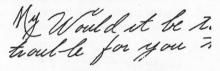

No. 26.   Frank, spiritually minded girl

No. 27 would have a life of trouble.   Coldness, calculation, selfishness
appear in the ending strokes of words.   The shading of the down
strokes shows self-indulgence, and the close-bound letters, meanness.

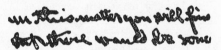

No. 27.   Cold-self-indulgent, mean

Even the t crossing gives a certain amount of brutality.   Men who
write in this fashion, showing these signs especially, do not make a
woman happy.

In No. 28, the extreme slope, the gross shading, flaring long letters
above the line, curved base line, all betray the same qualities.   The
minds of these writers are concentrated upon themselves and personal

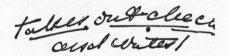

No. 28.   Dissipated, selfish

gratification.   Would any woman, though she were strongly attracted
toward a man, invite such a heartbreak, if she knew the traits that were
reflected by these signs?   Unfortunately there are some!

A writer who fashions his script, letters and words such as is found in No. 29, will be a fussy old tea-party, for the very careful, particular, exacting pen-prints, so fine and cramped, indicate the individual who would be like a hen on a hot griddle if he discovered an atom of dust on the lining of his last year's gumshoes, which were put away for the

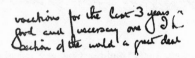

No. 29.   Fussy old tea party

Salvation Army.   This type generally drives a woman with sentiment or imagination into hysteria, religious movements, or, in fact, anything which will take her away from home.   And the strange thing is that, in numerous cases, this type of writer is chosen by a woman of the above class.   It may not be so in the future!

If you care for freedom from jealousy, worry, extravagance, irregular living, don't ally your fortunes with any person who writes like No. 30.   Like all his class, he will be magnetic, jolly, artistic, more or less of a genius, witty and daring.   But what an existence you would

No. 30.   Magnetic, daring, extravagant

lead!   His heart and head wobble—the angle of the writing changes to some extent.   Generous to a fault one minute—wide spaces between lines, words and letters; selfish the next—abrupt final endings and heavy shading of down strokes combined; and his open g and o signify that his glib tongue could roll off excuses as easily as rain falls from the skies.   He rounds his letters, and throws his h high in the air, indicating a vivid imagination. So he could softsoap anyone with whom he came in contact. Music and art are his gifts—he rounds his letters at the bottom, with heavy shading. Let him have his own way. His t bar shows he will take it in spite of you.

Though many things and reasons regulate a woman's choice of a helpmeet, in like manner as a man's, when the leading signs are similar with both her fiancé and herself, harmony will usually prevail. When the script is absolutely dissimilar—style, letters individual peculiari-

No. 31.   Idealistic, sincere, loves home life

ties and shading—quicksands and shoals are sure to be ahead. For example: Marry the writers of Nos. 31 and 32 together. The first is a woman of refinement and delicacy. The slope of her writing shows she is idealistic, sincere, a lover of home life, not wasteful or given to gad-

No. 32.   A gadabout

ding about. She has high standards to which she tries to adhere. In common with her companion, she has a love of music, which is practically the only point of interest. On the other hand, from the restlessness shown by the change in the direction of his words, indicating fickleness, and the irregular shading—the sign of a love of material pleasure—he would find it a task to stay at home. He is also extravagant—note the way the pen flows across paper and distance between lines. Hers is entirely different, as anyone can see. There is normality! Balance and even temperament are in the strokes.

Wedlock is a source of contentment and joy where the mind and physique are in tune. And to take any step of such vital importance as marriage, where evidences of bodily or nervous weakness appear, is most unwise. No. 33 is a fair example of a young man who has taxed his constitution to the limit. Naturally possessed of a powerful frame—

No. 33.   Naturally strong constitution, weakened

observe the heavy pressure and the length of the y's below the lines—the nervous t crossing, declining script and erratic dotting of the i in "it," mirrors a physical condition due to athletic overtraining, bringing about heart weakness. This shows in the break in the cross stroke in g in "glad." He expects to marry shortly, and the result will be, possibly, an invalid husband on the wife's hands.

Marriage may be considered an investment which pays large and cumulative dividends, provided men and women do not allow their judgment to be swamped by impulse. Examine your fiancé's script; it will pay you. The same holds with your acquaintances or friends. True marriages are supposed to be made in heaven, but it is reasonable to make sure that the contracts are properly written on earth so that the ideal may be attained.

I am frequently asked whether a child's writing shows any special tendencies, either as regards character or temperament, talent or the reverse. I have found it to be the case, especially where children are permitted to write naturally. The vertical hand, when learned, is modified later as a child develops and shows the effects of individuality. Will-power, judgment and affection, generosity or the opposite, and talent for music, show as early as seven years, and sometimes earlier. Good health is also denoted.

As illustrative, No. 34 was written by a child when twelve years old. You will note the same rounding sweep in the letters at the bottom, a like shading, and that the t bars are similar to those in No. 35 —the same individual at sixteen. But what a difference! The Greek

Mother and I wen todaz and we ha

No. 34.   Child writing "school hand"

e appears even in the first, when the writer was a mere kiddie. It is seen also in the second, showing the latent desire for self-improvement, which developed later as the strength and individuality of the writing

Ker than it did saved you from

No. 35.   The same at age 16, showing development

betrays. The a's and o's are open at the top alike. The capital M in "Mother" gives the natural force which this child possesses from the start, even though he is employing the "school hand." The long strokes in each, below the base line, show the physical vitality.

One who follows this line of work has frequently to act as a guide or familiar friend although he may not know his correspondents apart, except from their letters. A recent experience of this kind reveals the confidence and trust placed by a mother who required some practical suggestions to help and forward her child's interests, and secure harmony in the family.

No. 36 shows a portion of her letter. Her son, a young fellow about eighteen, had broken loose from the family, stayed out late at night,

and was obstinate and insolent. His father wished him to take up a
certain line of work but he wished to go into something else. Because

No. 36.   Portion of a mother's letter of distress

he was not permitted to follow his own bent—engineering—he refused
to obey his parents' wishes.

No. 37 is the boy's. His script, like his father's, slants to the right,
showing that each has much affection at heart. But both show stub-

No. 37.   The boy who was wayward. It shows that he
had much affection at heart

bornness and a determination to hold on to their point of view. This is
indicated by the heavy down strokes and blunted cross strokes. The

No. 38.   The father's handwriting. He is stubborn

high t bar denotes that the lad has a high temper. No. 38—the father's —shows a greater degree of stubbornness; the p in "prize" is almost club-shaped. Further, he is less impulsive, shown by the partly vertical slope. These signs denote that their wills would naturally clash.

After making an analysis, the following suggestions were given: "Let the boy act independently and pursue his own inclination. Do not criticize him but find out what his ambitions are. Sympathize with him in regard to his desires. The upward swing to the right shows that he is ambitious and not lazy." Similar advice was given to the mother, but from a different point of view. Her a's and o's are open at the top, indicating that she is too outspoken. Also the extreme slope signifies that her affection would cause her to be too anxious; she had to overcome a tendency to ask questions. Her boy was growing to manhood—perhaps she had not realized it. The outcome has proved satisfactory. The suggestions offered were accepted; harmony now reigns, and from the latest report the son is making good in the line of work which he has chosen. He stays home nights and studies persistently. This is only one case out of many.

Children will appreciate, to a greater degree, what their fathers and mothers are doing for their advancement, if they are taught that their writing shows just what they are.

If these few words and interpretation are of assistance to the readers I shall be doubly repaid for my efforts.

CHAPTER XVII

WHEN CUPID STARTS A-LAUGHING WITH HIS PEN AND INK

IN this day and generation, Dr. Cupid, President of the International Love Agency, has his hands full. He shoots his arrows and they return laden with problems which threaten to deprive him of his world-wide position and salary.

To unveil a few personalities in Screendom by an examination of their pen-prints will furnish many a clue to the reasons why certain types of writing should marry as a permanent passional investment, or the reverse. Temperament, harmonious disposition and tastes are the leading men and women in this variable drama of life. To discern these traits is easy, if you do not psycho-analyze what you hope or rather expect them to be and act, behind the celluloid colorful tapestries.

Affection and love from the standpoint of handwriting have as many sign-phases as there are styles of makeup. Love presents its incarnadined lips, translating by a mere touch to the lover some hoped for idea of permanency, exploding the powdered cheek to flame for a life-time. "Bunk! Punk!" exclaim our scornful critical parrots.

I confess it is rather ticklish business to describe the emotions and feelings of any man or woman when it comes to the selection of a side partner. But my own handwriting shows that I have the courage of my convictions. So here goes! Besides, some of these screen stars enjoy getting a tip on the market. So all they have to do here is to read the quotations of this particular stock ticker correctly.

Therefore we will turn on the calcium and use the microscope to see how far these writers will commit themselves. It is quite within the bounds of reason, if you will regard the firmly written, upright, well-poised script of Wanda Hawley, No. 1, to state that she will always use

No. 1.

her mind and keen wits; then in directing and displaying her affections. She applies herself with much perseverance and discriminating taste in the choice of a lover who would have to show that he could attract by having some emotional investment worth careful consideration and lasting. Her small letters are pointed at the top. Her eyes are wide-open and expectant. Having once made a selection, she would hold her male opportunity, employing every art in her power to make him a permanent addition to her bungalow. Swinging along with graceful rounded gait, she adapts herself to all of his moods and tenses. But not far or too often. Too shrewd for that! Her wisdom lies in knowing her man must be kept guessing.

There are no erratic sky-scraping, extravagant curves, indicating a temperament so flushed with intensity that she would be carried off her feet and into the Little Church Around the Corner willy-nilly. Not she! Still the caveman style appeals to her imagination, but that is as far as it would go. Hauling in her sails she would sit back in comfort, drifting along, letting her eyes pick out some canoeist who is athletic enough and sufficiently strong in character to assist her to make her goals. As briefly formed as are her finals, so she would hold herself aloof for a while. Then with beckoning hand or eye, she would get—very busy indeed! But not with the type of writer such as Bryant

Washburn, although to her mind's eye, he might possess attractive points. No. 2.

You will observe that in many features these two stars present a similar pen makeup. But even though their tastes and inclinations are alike, still they are really a testy pair of Heavenly twins in disposition

No. 2.

and affection. Within shooting distance in time, on their honeymoon, they would bore each other full of holes. Each would try the amiable stunt of smiling. And here you are! In their capitals are found that trace of self-esteem and lofty sensitiveness which would rear up in disgruntled fashion, driving one to the road in a motor car, perhaps, the other to a new scenario. Neither would eventually show any wild desire to get off the personal pedestal. Would this pair come under the wire in the matrimonial race at the same time? Quite so! Quite so! For the inherent demand to win first in artistic work would sooner or later cause them to take different Pullmans to New York.

AND HOW ABOUT WALLIE?

And it is to be noted how the striking handwriting-trend of thought and action will introduce Wallace Reid, No. 3, as a type who, with his

No. 3.

rather remarkable style, distinctive, large and high-flung strokes would make a strong personal appeal to a woman of Wanda's calibre. He is "so devilishly" frank in his capacity for affection, coupled with a tender ardor which only might make itself felt by a slight touch of the hand, a quick glance—declaring much that might be said in words. But he is the foxy lad. See how he surrounds his real attitude by the broad lasso-curve of his capital "H." Underneath he has the real tendency to idealize, even idolize the object of his romantic feeling. The actuating motive to immediate action! He is innately responsive even to the small lift of the voice, to a casual gesture. But back of this is a self-conscious repression until he has the feeling that he is sure. "That is a deucedly attractive woman," is his first thought. His second, "I wonder if her ideas and tastes are like mine. Her appreciation of beauty." With restrained eagerness he will proceed to find out. He is a love educator. Will match coldness with apparent indifference, and then nonchalantly make the first move. After he had gotten his stride he would flush the game in the matter of loving, intelligently. His curved, rapid movement betrays that he is athletic when propelled by deep emotion. He will leap, so that he might—I say, might—sweep her off her feet.

Her head indignantly would flash, "Not on your life!" Her heart thumping fast, "I guess he's the man at last." With these two as with all others who write like them, there is a high degree of emotional glamour—one strong connecting link. They would disagree amicably. Both will give in after a little decoration of their real feelings. Each has enough common sense to talk over quietly—common cents. Her glance is for the future. His to spend recklessly on his mate. Should Wanda Hawley marry such a writer sooner or later she would give in to his individual likes and dislikes. There is a French adage which reads, "There is one who loves and one who is loved." Yet here there is sufficient balance for each to scratch gravel for the other. And the firmest bond is their love of outdoor life and the desire for personal improvement. But right now, the gods forbid that I make any claim to act as a suggestive obligato to any matrimonial love ditty. It is not my business in life, even if I do give a hint to those who can think beyond their noses.

For an entirely different reason, Bebe Daniels, No. 4, with her forceful, energetic, daring, independent temperament would attract Wallace Reid in the same fashion as an exotic who is to be admired, approached,

No. 4.

dangling for a brief moment, and then hurrah and away. Each of them! Every sweeping bold line in flight is vitally aflame, moving ahead impulsively with indifference to what others may really think. The original Bebe—note her "i" dotting and double understroke—is ingenious. So ingenious and deft that she handles the pantaloons so that they spell evening clothes, her male rushing dashingly forward until—laughingly she holds out her hand to the pussy-cat cops to let them know in what unexpected direction she is going. So if Bebe and Wallie married—well, they just wouldn't normally—there would be too much-a-muchness of a certain kind.

"Miauw, Miauw, Psst, Psst—," and Wallace quietly thinking sub rosa, "The next station for mine, if you please!" And beat it! But *of course* they would always be good friends. And Dr. Cupid would jamb his broken shaft into his quiver with "Oh, the devil! How did I ever get into the wrong pew. It must have been that clergyman assistant."

No. Bebe Daniels has to secure a better fate—a better handwriting complement than this. One that would understand how to stand under

and withstand.   Her individualistic artistic capitals invite her to
attract, to distract, to amuse, and perhaps even upset a writer who
takes himself with very great seriousness.   Sentiment clad in henna,
black and orange, or violet, rules her brain after all is said and done.
She is the kindly, generous sort who will intuitively see when her mate
was aweary, even though suffering herself, and hand him a selected
bouquet from her earnings, "just to be a good sport."   This is not a
tip, believe me, for those who do not write aright.

JOHN BARRYMORE BETTER YET!

Now among the wide variety of star-writers, I find but one who
really could hold her general impulses in leash, appeal to her and not
get fussed.   I am taking an editorial dare in introducing John Barrymore.   No. 5.   "Well, I'll be——.   Wouldn't that jar you!"   Yes, Miss

John Barrymore

No. 5.

Daniels, yes!   But shock absorbers have their uses on the highways of
marital adventure.   And this is just what John Barrymore is in the
fields of emotional and affectional experience.   His fine, though firm
delicacy in writing, sloping at the angle of over 45 degrees, his perfect
connections and minutely formed words, reveal a steady constancy and
affection unmarred by too intellectual or too temperamental streaks.
He thinks things over very seriously.

His simple art-wrought capitals enforce his usual calmness in personal emergencies.   His method of thought restrains his sentiment and
sensibilities.   So if he were allied to any woman he would seek for some
similarities of ideas and aspirations.   His quiet determination leads
him to use his head should his consort fly off the handle.   That blunt
final of his gives a steady hand at the conjugal wheel.   Hence, this is
what would happen with Miss Daniels.   He will stand pat—and pat
her hand if she became teary.   If the feminine vibrations started to run

amuck, well—after all he is an excellent shock absorber! There is one exception—if any woman tried to direct his ambitions, then it would be "Whooee!" for fair.

HOW ABOUT AGNES AYRES

Looking over my curios, I find that the writing of Agnes Ayres, No. 6, with her like slant, gracefully molded words somewhat shaded, her general easy balance, is the type who has all the hallmarks which would

No. 6.

match his own on the plane of the affections. In fact, her restraint in times of stress would help such a writer, her ambitious trend assisting him when he does not feel up to the high-water mark. She will use a tactful manner and adapt herself to any of his peculiar situations. Her widely sweeping capitals exhibit that pride which animates but does not destroy a home. True, she has a strong critical side and sense—she sharpens her small letters in spots—but will wish to use it for his benefit. But intelligently. He would have to praise her, always. These two types could match pennies continuously for their common good. And not scrap their warship!

IF CLYDE COOK AND IRENE CASTLE WERE!

"Dimes and dollars, dollars and dimes
An empty pocket is the worst of crimes,"

would be the bone of contention between Irene Castle and Clyde Cook, should this pair drag the halter from the altar. And Irene, No. 7, would

No. 7.

take the first large bite. Not that she shows any giddy proscenium lights in the matter of real economy. She would expect expectantly plenty of the coin which was made round to go round, for instance. She has an upstanding script. Her head works by arithmetic. Her bold "t"-bar and blunt finals betray her positive conviction that she is right. "Why it is absurd to spend the way we do," she would reiterate stubbornly. All because she has chosen the wrong style of writer. So since Clyde, No. 8, inscribes a free, generous, happy-go-lucky fist, his capitals

No. 8.

sprawling in lively fashion, his "o's" being wide-open, he would probably respond with a cheerful laugh. "Don't know how it is, old girl, but I was born so. Besides, I must live up to my reputation. Here's a hundred."

"Thanks—awfully!" Then they would bill and coo a bit. For the real sentimental affectionate slope shows that at heart he is as tender and emotion-filling as a Delmonico steak broiled for ten minutes over old hickory. But what kind of a handwriting film do you expect from two persons so contradictorially amiable? Such screen writers are never attracted by any known law of gravitation, except possibly on Broadway. Do you wonder that each would seek another partner for the merry dance of life! Eventually!

CAROL DEMPSTER AND CECIL DE MILLE

The way of a man with a maid depends on their sentimental attitude —plus! So there are other inclinations and traits in handwriting which require the deft hand of a costumer for them to be exhibited here.

Again we find the heavy, fleet, boldly connected strokes of Cecil de Mille, No. 9, stretching their way upwards, betraying his utter devotion

No. 9.

to the dictates of his imagination as expressed in the terms of affections which must be fully gratified. An artist of life and no fool at trade, he would realize in his ideal a writer who had a light and even fantastic touch, whose charm and responsiveness would enchain by their many variations. And such is Carol Dempster, No. 10. Her very large script

No. 10.

talks to you in a lively fashion. Behold what high curves she prints in, her looped letters extending above her lines of thought, as gracefully as she would gesture with her hands. Imagination also. She handles herself with many a gracious mannerism designed to attract by a very illusive come-here-and-talk-to-me quality. De Mille does not like people to do things without permission, but would be as thrifty in his indignation as his intentional thrift, at times. Carol Dempster has that kind of a luxurious nature which enables her to find a way of spending her salary even before it has germinated. But his sentiment would choose this type of writing, anyhow. They would attract through their marked dissimilarities. He values any work of art. How much more a living creature vitalized by evasive individuality!

"Would they marry? How long would they live together?" Now, do not be in a hurry. I am not the clairvoyant stenographer! But this much I can say. Their penmanship reveals that they would have the happy faculty to agree to disagree. And if you want any closer bond in marriage than that, you will have to tell me.

THEN THERE'S DOROTHY DALTON AND HOUDINI

"This is a joke that is well worth the telling:
Shylock for Portia's gold his liberty is selling.
She on the crafty man her hand is bestowing,
We'll go to the wedding sure-ly,—GO—yes, we're—
G-O-I-N-G!"

All but the President of this love agency! Called upon to be best man at this particular function of Dorothy Dalton and Harry Houdini—and

No. 11.

he would go on a strike. No. 11. Not for any prejudice against either of them. But just because a woman who lifts her written capitalized head with such enormously shaded curves, crosses her "t's" with such fine decision, her letters with such energy, would be very likely to lead her husband straight from the altar with a determination to make him show his love with many gestures. She has the brains to get what she wants. Her affectional disposition demands an object who will ring the chimes, yesterday, today and—

Harry Houdini

No. 12.

Well, Houdini would start in finely. No. 12. He would worship at her shrine. Every rounded and original stroke exudes his desire to please. He would never wobble unless he had to toss over his pay envelope. He is the type who needs more than thirty cents to quench his thirst. Strong, deliberate, he walks slowly across his sentimental pages with an ingenious thoughtful mien. His thoughts would be long, long gasps of mental query if any question of his attentions were criticised. And Dorothy Dalton demands many attentions. No fault of hers! Every line and even height of small letters reveal his desire to be constant. But, perhaps fortunately for him, that lassoed stroke below his signature acts as a sign of a clever fashion of extricating himself from tight places. So with this type of writer, he would come to the conclusion that he must get out. Beat it, fast.

But after all she would do the deciding. No slick slacker for hers. "The idea of his being so cold. I have my work also. H-m-m-m!"

And then he would retire muttering joyously, "Hurrah for the Irish and the devil take the Dutch." While she sits back in her limousine, her shoulders looming up as high as her script, annoyingly fussed by having "such a wasted emotional experience. Girls, I just do not know how I came to marry that man." She would know if she knew

anything about handwriting.   Tom Mix could make her stand around
—has the emotional grip in his hands.

> *"Home sweet home, home sweet home!*
> *How we love the Sabbath School.*
> *Bless the teachers of the Sabbath School!"*

And so we go merrily on.

CHAPTER XVIII

THE SUCCESS OF FAVORITE MOVIE STARS EXPLAINED IN THEIR HAND-
WRITING

THERE is no thumb-rule to measure success. It rests upon the intelligence, force and personality of the individual. To one, special endowments are given that seem to enhalo the writer with a vivid and unique quality. To another, that magnetic power which emanates from beauty, grace and emotional expression, contributing to the highest achievement in this the silent drama.

Actions speak louder than words, and those shown in the signatures of these screen stars have a peculiar significance when we examine closely the variety of their pen-reflections. For each writer as persuasively attracts by special pressure, curves or other strokes as by any other external characteristics. More so, in fact, since each formation furnishes particular evidence of the writer's thoughts, actions, ambitions and other tendencies. So I shall open each letter of introduction in the signature and read the hidden meaning underlying the individual's purpose as expressed in successful accomplishment. Each star shines from within outward, compelling by sheer electric attraction.

ELSIE FERGUSON

Now when Elsie Ferguson No. 1, inscribed her name, she voiced that she is glowing with vitality, intensity, vigorous activity, with the determination and fertile imagination necessary to light her way towards the realization of every ambition. She travels forcefully upwards. Each stroke is firmly imbedded on the paper showing that she emphatically declares to herself that she will be successful. Nothing will interfere. The grace exhibited in her capitals, original and aviating into the blue, her lofty looped "L," merely emphasizes that her vision

No. 1.

guides her imaginatively to vitalize each character she portrays. The long, extended stroke below the line exclaims physical strength and endurance to withstand all assaults upon her emotions. She reflects in color and intensity each passing phase, each feeling, as the shading of her letters are equally pronounced. A curve is the line of beauty. Her individual curves are numerous. Some letters sharpened at the top reveal a disposition to secure what she desires with subtle stubbornness backed up by conviction that she is right. How she will fight to gain her point. But persuasively with buoyant adaptability. So with her success means the development of her own personality in the active virile expression of herself.

GEORGE ARLISS

A strong intellect, rapid methods of thinking, alertness and dominating energy are hallmarked by the pen-forms of Arliss. No. 2. Stimulated by a firm will to attain the goal he sets out to attain, he never hesitates to make his decision quickly. He paces his steps with unflinching courage—a courage inspired by an exaltation of spirit and imagination fine and clear, so that he never fails to impress upon his workmanship the stamp of delicate artistry, of creative power. His high extensions

No. 2.

above the line, his dominating sweeping capital "S" are finished exhibits. Self-confidence, nervous excitation and originality are permanent traits. How emphatic is his gesture below his signature!

This affirms his power of application shown by his low connected letters. An occasional curve shows his reserved geniality. Withal his pointed style betrays a grim cynicism, a humor variable and even biting. Sentiment rules his daily life. With such characteristics is there any doubt he succeeds in a versatile fashion? Still he takes himself seriously—always. The keynote in the gamut of his varied outlook is his intellectual grasp in interpreting life.

SHIRLEY MASON

The light, delicately shaded impressions of Shirley Mason, No. 3, swinging gracefully in curved fashion to the right, are a revelation of buoyant ambition, adaptability, and a lively interest in all that she thinks

No. 3.

and does. Deftly she colors her strokes, lassoing her ideas with the high loops of her "h" and "l." These two tell of rapid speech, of gaiety in verbal expression. Words link themselves together. She is frank, knows her own mind and thinks things out. That she is stubborn at odd moments, will stand pat, and needs to be persuaded, appear in her sharp-pointed down stroke below the line. Pride in her own ability, her own progress, her ease to fill her rôles, is found in her capital "M." For this reason she will never let up to make good. Understanding merely a hint, she will follow a suggestion with artistic comprehension. In temperament she is a bit changeable, but not a wild creature untamed! Sensitive to criticism, but endowed with common sense as well. Her style denotes her versatility which enables her to throw a spell over others. But such a sentimentalist!

WILLIAM FARNUM

By contrast, the striking, virile, decisive script exhibited by William Farnum, No. 4, indicates directness of aim and determined energy which carries him steadily along to achieve his ends. Each stroke is forceful,

No. 4.

while his well-made connections show his ability to reason and not falter in keeping faith with himself. None can influence him against his will. He holds tightly to what he has in mind, having a belief in himself. That he forms his capitals with a certain high distinction, with a strong crossbar, merely asserts that meeting an obstacle he will leap over it. The fine clutch at the end of his last letter means that he has tenacity of purpose. It may not appear on the surface since his general disposition is agreeable, even though he has the fighting quality. He has that kind of shrewd intelligence which guides him to a complete comprehension of the work at hand. Goes after it steadily. There is nothing wobbly in his temperament. Too vital! Through his emotional perceptions, his insight, he is able to make his points appreciated by both men and women. The sense of sentimental values, is strong. Too strong at times. Persistent endeavor is the keystone to his character structure.

MARGUERITE CLARK

The embodiment of a sunny, genial, enthusiastic disposition, buoyed up by optimism, is Marguerite Clark, No. 5, whose vision leads her to picture in advance what she has to undertake, and then she holds on

No. 5.

with a competent idea that she will win through. Sensitive and responsive to color and music, to any adverse criticism, she will throw herself into her work enthusiastically, provided praise is given. Her lofty capitals proclaim her keen enjoyment in doing things well, due to her enormous pride.

Her personal vivacity, coupled with her flow of talk, attracts friends to her as well as others. Her pen-style reflects her determination to dominate through studied charm, which is also natural. Does she save money? She does not if she can help it. She is generous, impulsively so. Those backward curves of her final letters match her ability to smile. Likewise there is an April-like touch of temper—impatience. "A good fellow." Her capacity for emotion is right on the job. So her signature is saying, "Here take me." And then laugh.

TOM MIX

Here we find a new and dashing type. Tom Mix, No. 6, whose handwriting is full of daring, resourcefulness, energy, recklessness and the ability to mind his own business. He thinks and acts on his feet and

No. 6.

talks straight to the point. Lively and active. He never stops until he finishes even in a whirlwind. Has the instinct for unexpected laziness. His is the quality for salesmanship. His vision is practical. But he will stick to the last throw if he believes that the gift of the gods is coming his way. A real combination of sentiment and hardy romance with the salt and pepper of new experience necessary. He curves his elongated strokes with large letters—quick in all emergencies! He is pleasant and offhand generally, with that degree of temperament which carries him ahead to any or all situations. That flamboyant circular connection between his two names invites you to borrow money from him if you know how. His inky expression is redundant with that energetic character which makes for individual achievement—and successfully.

NAZIMOVA

To translate the varied emotions which flash through the alert intelligence of Nazimova, No. 7, can only be told in part. One glance at her large heavily-shaded and original style, her immense capital N and bold underscoring, will convince anyone that here is a unique and daring personality who flames forth on her ambitious path as some brilliant exotic. No one can really control her. She controls others in

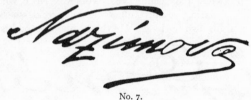

No. 7.

the same fashion as she holds herself splendidly genial, then at times coldly aloof, but always bearing her presence with supreme confidence. Responsive to color, beauty, melody, she luxuriates in blending her impressions into many creative lines. Seizing a fresh idea, she studies it until it becomes a living thing. As firm as her heavy sharp writing are her convictions and beliefs. Her will-power is twin to her energy and sensuous gifts. They are the leading features which attract to her by their sheer electric exuberance the best that the world can offer. Nevertheless, she is a Madame Sans Gêne, as to her independence.

Just in passing, if Nazimova and Tom Mix married there would be wars and rumors of wars. Just two different temperaments!

WALLACE REID

If you will note the steady facile flow, rounded, firm handwriting of Wallace Reid, No. 8, you will get the leading clue to his smooth-

No. 8.

working intellect, distinctive individuality, and positive actions. No vacillation or hesitancy! He is direct, candid and adaptable, having a mannerly manner. He does not "fly kites" at suggestions. But goes on and on with a steady sort of quiet determination.

There is a bonhomie, a light artistic touch with finished details so that intelligence is manifest all through. And this apart from his professional work. Reserved—and then a good mixer! He understands both men and women—and that also tells a big story. As his personal pride and self-assurance are large, so he handles himself with aplomb. He has a sensitive nerve. He may enjoy the plaudits of the multitude, but at home will doff the adulations or what not, satisfied to be away. Persistent and consistent, he ignores the temporary successes for the larger accomplishment where he feels that he counts in a large way.

BILLIE BURKE

Out of the skies there falls occasionally a human being whose penformations, curved, light and dark, positive yet flexible, which always reveal a facile personality. Such a one is Billie Burke, No. 9. With only

No. 9.

half an eye, you can sense the frankness, simplicity and liveliness in her style. Her capital B's are full of artistic appreciation, color and jollity, as if she said, "Oh, yes I am all of that and more." Backward under her signature is the bold strong double line accentuating her whole attitude towards life—agreeable and interesting development of her power through intelligent work. She does not stop to consider the whys and wherefores but just forges ahead, for she breaks her letters somewhat apart, being very intuitive and inspirational. She knows her line of success because she has ever felt it. And does. Con-

14

sequently she tries to please—always. Little gusts of temper, yes! But her affections are deep-seated and lasting. She holds people through an intrinsic innate faculty which is founded upon her intuition. Personality plus!

WILLIAM S. HART

Where an individual has the brain to conceive a definite aim in life and then stick to it, you find the pressure strong, decisive, with balance and steady movement throughout. And William S. Hart, No. 10, has

No. 10.

all of these pen-traits and more. He firmly strides uphill with his solid slant, his bold t-bar bearing obstinately to the right. His capital letters are normally proportional to the small ones, each being formed as if he meant business and intended to stay with it. Here and there he stops between letters to reflect and plan, to secure new light to illumine his subsequent actions. The simplicity of his capitals is the sign of his own real simplicity of life. Each final stops short—reserve! But there is also reserve force which is courage and deliberate daring, when you ally his clearcut words, and poised! His is the critical eye and mind. Letters are sharp at the top! And because his signature is balanced throughout he shows executive ability. His is the success which comes through a definite aim and action.

Fame has many fans. To be famous signifies the recognition of some sort of success achieved. And no surer fashion of determining the essential elements which make for high popular acclaim can be found than that which an individual exhibits in handwriting. So when you regard the signatures of screen stars, you are looking squarely at the high or low lights switched on by the electrical currents of their personalities. The steady glow holds your attention. The power underneath you feel even if you do not know the cause. For this reason, if for no other, there is a wide demand for the personally-written signatures of men and women prominent in this expression of the drama. Likewise, upon the signature, every writer unconsciously places great stress in using certain strokes that declare the prominent traits. Handwriting is the natural private gesture of each person's whole makeup, and you will see that it only requires the eye and the mind working together to form a fair judgment.

CONSTANCE TALMADGE

So in the minute and a half when Constance Talmadge, No. 11, was writing her name, she unconsciously put herself on record as a woman whose physical exuberance and love of action, health, trend of mind and

No. 11.

energy, furnish her with considerable balance and poise. Her brain is alive with ideas, notions, warmed and flushed by a happy way of looking at life, temperamentally cheerful and laughter-loving. Still no amount of detailed work robs her of the pleasure of doing everything with a finished gesture.

She will say to any adverse criticism, "Well, I've done my best. Do you want more than that, for Heaven's sake?" Which shows that she enjoys using her wits and a bit of henna-toned temper. But only occasionally. In her comings and goings among her associates she moves calmly, easily, with even a half-indifferent air. Her capitals reach upwards as if to grasp some bigger thing upon which to lay the impress of her whole self.   Here is her pride, her belief in a sun-lit future.   She is reliable.   Loyal—but a bit distrustful.   She really admits few into intimate companionshlp.   Her affections are potent, but her humorous eye would seize the amusing side of anyone who tried to be serious in a motor car.   "Stop, look, listen," oh ye of the opposite sex!   And she uses her brains always.   Thus she is human enough to hold any material advantage as a cemented flight of stairs upon which she intends to tread steadily in aiming for the best in creative work.

RODOLPH VALENTINO

In the same healthy atmosphere travels R. Valentino, No. 12, whose even, well-poised fist moves ambitiously upwards, gesturing with his rather flamboyant capitals, exclamatory of his intense vitality and the

No. 12.

conscious belief in himself.   Each carefully-connected stroke invites you to look into his active mind, teeming with an intense desire to make good.   In each curve lurks a laugh.   In the straight base-line, strengthened by the long, underscoring sweep, he assures you frankly that he has a great deal of nerve and will never be satisfied until you meet him frequently.   That bold hook on the end of his "t" shows his grit, his clinching hold on every detail in order to produce in a versatile manner with artistic finesse.   The way he gathers his letters together—a clutch —denotes his practical side.   Once attempt to worst him by any ill-treatment and his whole temperament will arise with an adequate come-back.   It would surprise you, as he is tactful and pleasing in manner.   By nature vitally strong, he is the type who will meet flame with flame and enter into the gaiety of living.   Yet, pressure being even, he understands the art of self-dominance. By this his advance along the stellar way can be measured by the height of his signature. Very high.

GLORIA SWANSON

"No possible probable shadow of doubt, no possible doubt whatever," that the immensely virile swing, well-balanced style with curvilinear capitals shown by Gloria Swanson, No. 13, gives evidence that

No. 13.

she possesses a vigorous personality. She is able to adapt herself to any new conception or situation, exhibiting a staying-power constant and lively. That lofty looped "l," combined with the long-curved pen-gait, tells of a frank, straightforward person who has a rapid speech, positive and clean-cut, while her fondness for rhythm and melody would be apparent in every pose, every gesture. A great love of beauty, music, and the wide open spaces causes her to think and act in the terms of nature and action. Still, having a dual personality, there is a luxurious appreciation of everything that can be offered in the way of enjoyment. An existence which winds and curves through the purlieus of light and even excitement, has an allure for her. So she gains in experience and responsiveness, being able to interpret them in her own fashion.

Actually emotion is one dominant keynote, the emotion which holds her through her picturesque vision. There is never any relaxation when she views ahead of her—big achievement. That long extended outward final ending is a positive, emphatic exclamation that she is tireless to attain her goals.

TOM MEIGHAN

An excellent letter of introduction is the signature of Thomas Mei-
ghan, No. 14, whose slightly vertical script, firm pressure throughout,
and perfect connecting strokes denote his active intelligence, self-control

No. 14.

and assurance, in all emergencies. He has the determination to put
things through despite any obstacles. He brings his positive bold
extending stroke below the line in a masterly fashion, indicating his
power of maintaining his point of view without yielding. Still, his
rounded even flow reveals his disposition to be considerate and generally agreeable. Not liable to go out of his way to antagonize anyone,
even though independence of character is markedly stated. His is the
practical vision which enables him to plan and execute, for he has
executive ability, tried or untried. Those who know him realize his
personal reserves, his tendency to be close-mouthed concerning his
private affairs. There is a sharp wit, even caustic at times. But this
is not a high light of his general character. In the performance of any
special assignment, his reliability and responsibility would be patent.
The large, though simple style inscribed, taken with his high, well-
constructed capital "M," enforces his tenacity of purpose, his aims,
with constant pride. A stable personality.

BARBARA CASTLETON

The upright, easy-swinging pen-gait of Barbara Castleton, No. 15,
with the large appearance of her letter-formations, are a revelation of a
clear, active mind and an adaptable and friendly attitude. No matter in

what position she might find herself, she has the wit to extricate herself. Kindly and full of reserved power, she enters into the spirit of affairs readily, easily. No perpetual chip on her shoulder! When she barred

No. 15.

her "t" with the little clutch at the end and the blunted form of her finals, she answers in a semi-jovial fashion, "Oh, I am able to take care of myself all right. I can keep my end up."

BUCK JONES

"There, I guess that will do," is the remark Buck Jones, No. 16, lets forth in a haphazard fashion, when he dashed off his name. The rapid, forceful slant upwards to the right photographs clearly his opti-

No. 16.

mistic, buoyant nature. He holds one definite idea in his mind—to get there by every possible effort. The fairly heavy pressure reinforced by the long, sweeping, curved stroke of his "J" is the semaphore flashing physical activity, great endurance, recklessness and courage, in all lines of endeavor. Let anyone dare him to take any risk and he will never hesitate. Socially he is a good mixer with a frank, open nature. But even at that he has a curious fashion at keeping his own counsel.

DORIS KENYON

Dash, fire, gaiety, cheerfulness and a tremendous desire to become a thorough workman in the line of artistic endeavor, are the leading pentraits of Doris Kenyon, No. 17.   She dashes across the page with an ex-

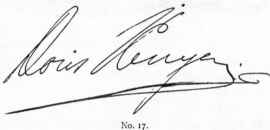

No. 17.

altation of spirit, enthusiasm, having as persistent a will and unflagging energy as the elongated "t" crossings shout aloud.   Just try to interfere with this writer's fertile ideas or actions, and you will retire from her location post-haste.   Like a barbed-wire fence, her sharpened style protects her and strengthens her convictions and opinions.   There is a steady devotion to her friends, and oddly enough she does not care a rap if there are people who do not like her.   A belief that she will attain her end anyhow and independently!   Colorful is her script and shaded, a revelation of high ability to reflect emotion and feeling in any situation, professional or otherwise.   She does love appreciation and praise. It is the salad of her existence.   She has initiative and courage.   Impulsive?   Yes, indeed.

JACK HOLT

The distinctive form and character portrayed by Jack Holt, No. 18, with his original unique capitals and rigid down strokes, indicate a personality strongly prominent in his ability to attract attention.   A written lode-stone, having a brain which functions keenly, and a mind

alert to grasp all opportunities. The power in his positively shaded
pressure reflects his decisive trend to get things. After he initialed his
first name, he stopped with a quick breath—reflection and a certain

No. 18.

canny fashion of visualizing his ideas or mental pictures so that actually
he can make them count in the terms of accomplishment. He has a
sense of values, an excellent analytical method of dissecting each bit of
work, and then applying a finished touch to his own interpretation.

MARY PICKFORD

"Mary, Mary, quite contrary, how does your garden grow?" is a
quotation which expresses one side of the character of Mary Pickford,
No. 19, for in every positive down-stroke in her signature and carefully-

No. 19.

formed vertical letters, she is insistent that her own ideas and rights
shall, at least, be given every consideration.

Sensitive pride always arrives to her rescue—pride in creating
artistic things, in finished workmanship. She senses the value of new
ideas intuitively and holds them with a grip. But as each word is

curved with a delicately deliberate movement, upstanding on a pedestal as it were, she will yield gracefully when she feels that she has to. And never otherwise.   In personal and intimate affairs she would never know when she was beaten.   Her original capital "P" is an invitation to regard her as fairly and squarely a person who really knows what she is about—with a strong undercurrent of will-power to work and work with large industry.   There is little subtlety.   Frank and straightforward, but can dodge an issue occasionally with deliberation.   You will not catch her napping, believe me.   Her type of writing exhibits a love of nature, animals, music and certain kinds of excitement.   But discreet with her excitements.   She demands freedom for the expression of her own individuality and gets it.   And will!   To her success is the major theme upon which she weaves her life.   Oddly enough, her tastes and pleasures are simple.

DOUGLAS FAIRBANKS

"I don't **care a damn**" is the characteristic offhand expression of thought as shown by the holograph written by Douglas Fairbanks.   No. 20.   His intellect works with intensity, reinforced by his dominant con-

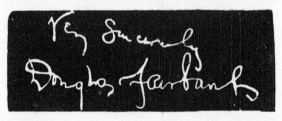

No. 20.

tinuous pressure and club-like formations descending below his lines with little curlicues.   A combination of reserved force, endurance, daring and wit.   You cannot fease this writer.   Note his very low small letters pointed at the top with frequent stopping points in his words.

Shrewd to the nth degree! Penetration and the ability to scheme and plan are his traits. He executes with a certain kind of domination which he assumes is all right.

Still the originality shown in many combined strokes, curves abounding throughout, signify his genial temperament. But, Lord, how very cross he can be occasionally! He is a happy alliance of thrift and extravagance. Although he is dashingly exuberant, with it is a susceptible nature—one sensitive! But he does not show this openly. Consummate nerve is his animating tendency, while his impulses propel him naturally to take all kinds of chances just for the devilment of it. Each extraordinary capital and looped letter strives to reveal his varied kinds of imagination and intellectual fertility. Actually he is nowhere near as commercial as some people may delight to believe. His success is due to an electric current which is turned on everlastingly. His individuality drives him to do and work for definite ends—vigorously.

In this group of pen-personalities, the reader will observe how each individual expresses the interior force which bears each one to some particular goal. To some particular niche largely self-constructed! So from the widely varied types as far as written information is concerned, it is possible to compare the writing of others with the above and then glean whether actual screen star elements are present. And if so, stop and reflect. And if not so—why, it is up to you!

CHAPTER XIX

PSYCHOLOGICAL SURVEYS

Cosmo Hamilton's Written Personality

THE pen-personality of every individual is the measure of his intensive intellectual force. The nerves pulsating through the hand

Facsimile of Cosmo Hamilton's Handwriting

reflectively direct the action of his conscious and unconscious mind. So Mr. Cosmo Hamilton, when he uses his pen, reveals the high peak to which his distinctive personality extends.

The calm, even, steady and deliberate flow reinforced by his firm pressure and well-wrought connecting strokes indicates a virile intellect, continuity of thought and immense power of application. He possesses the will to achieve and does not hesitate until he has accomplished his purpose, has reached his goal. No vacillation, no febrile indecision!! His high heavy "t" crossings declare that he will make a decision and adhere to it. His convictions are positive, being cemented into a stubborn rock of determination and naught will affect his ideas if he feels that he is right. He gathers his letters together as with a closed fist, while his finals stop short! A man of great and many reserves which will even show in his manner of speaking and acting. Here and there a "t"-bar dashes to the right—he was born with his eyes wide open, alert in close observation which enables him vividly to portray whatever he visualizes. Imagination clear and untrammeled! Thus his words run off his pen in minute concentrated form with "l's" and "t's" extending well above the line.

So when Cosmo Hamilton stops, making frequent breaks between letters, with original artistic connections, he offers the evidence that he works under a fine-drawn inspiration, his ideas leaping forth into consciousness with the creative impulse teeming underneath. Likewise, his capitals are simple, graceful, many of them print-like in formation. An artist who handles his tools with ease, deftly, and almost unconsciously! His senses are alert, while his intuition inspires him to a complete understanding of both men and women, although women are his métier. His signature declares it.

The Handwriting of Mildred Cram

Unto the gifted intellectually is handed by destiny the art of expressing their ideas with the same ingenuity and originality in which they form their written style with artistically shaded capitals and unique connections. So this writer impresses upon you her attractive, buoyant personality, revealing a quick live intelligence animated by a forceful virile imagination and a keen responsiveness to beauty in all of its forms.

With her mind wide-open, she gathers in her impressions, she reconstructs her visions so that they are alive with vitality—and intensely real. As her hand forms the lightly shaded words and letters,

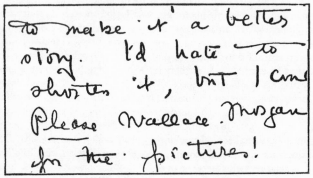

Facsimile of Mildred Cram's Handwriting

stopping now here, now there, between words, she unfolds the process of her mind in pouring forth her creations. Reflective yet intuitive, she proceeds by inspiration, as though she had listened to some transcendent spirit who whispered to her the secrets of color and illusive form. And spontaneously she immediately understands the hidden meaning and then translates into life her intimate impressions. Curling up the corners of her mouth in the same whimsical fashion in which she twists backward some of her finals—she smiles or even laughs and finishes her ideas with rapid stroke and fleet application.

For to her is given the ability to insinuate her way alluringly through her rounded, adaptable, pleasant nature into the hearts and companionship of others.

And to her lively sympathies there is an undercurrent of eager ambition, of a willingness to criticize her own ideas so that they will present to others their truth and simple accuracy. For her images are never distorted by any bizarre conception, by any flamboyancy that will mislead by its temperamental suggestions. She thinks as directly as she carries herself straight in all of her actions. That she moves across the page with an almost transparent honesty is shown by the lines. No sinuosity or deliberate holding together her letters or words in too close liaison! So it is possible to say of her that she will ever give of her best and highest inspirations, reveal the inner processes and motives—candidly. When she throws her long looped letters high above the line —her signature—she says that she always intends to be intellectually honest and broadminded. "Most certainly, I have a little human vanity," she will laugh. "See how I stretch out my capital M way up in the clouds."

Chirographic Survey of Monsieur Erté

The dream life of a man wherein his dreams become virile clear realities is portrayed by the original and striking inscriptions made by

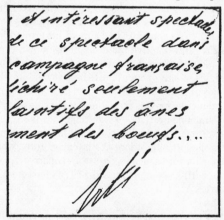

Facsimile of Erté's Handwriting

Monsieur Erté in writing. Stroke by stroke, artistically, he displays in each letter standing forth by itself, his vivid imagination, fecund and aflame with new conceptions, fresh ideas, the value of which he intuitively grasps. And then with a steady intensity of purpose, as steady as the crossings of his "t's," he proceeds to brush into reality his thoughts, simply but with brilliant chiaroscuro. And in the clear strong light of inspiration his vision creates new forms as colorful as the delicate shading of each word.

And for this reason he delights in paradox, his intellect responsive to the promptings of his imagination, to the stimulus of rhythm and melody in every realm of art. He lives with his dreams as with vitalized personalities. His gradual slope to the right endows him with sentiment of an intense character which dominates while it inspires. And under the vivid light of his feelings and emotions, he will both idolize and idealize the object of his affections.

So under the influence of the sheer joy of living he vibrates perhaps too intensely and suffers through a fine sensitiveness, both to criticism and any lack of comprehension. By each capital letter, curved, somewhat flamboyant, he expresses this sensitive attitude.

As Monsieur Erté is emphatic and sure of his ground in all that he does, as he has a shrewd active mind, he brings down firmly his pen-gestures. It is doubtful whether anyone can persuade him to alter his modus vivendi, his modus operandi. He believes in himself.

The little things count and the fact that he is so careful in forming his meticulous punctuation, his precise and immaculate style, is merely his fashion of announcing that his workmanship is finished—the reflection of his personality. And in the rapid high ascending strokes of his signature is the lofty ambition, the intensive force which helps to throw his personality into a niche separate and apart—a place where he wills to operate with a strong independence of character. Individual to the nth degree!

The Handwriting of Josephine Daskam Bacon

In our American realm of literature, ofttimes there flashes a pen-personality that is distinctive with force and an abounding current of imagination. And as such, Josephine Daskam Bacon expresses her intellectual virility with the rapid intense flow of her writing, while her high extensions above the line are united by words that speak aloud

Facsimile of Josephine Daskam Bacon's Handwriting

with color and feeling. Her conceptions spring forth fully armed from a mental reservoir overflowing with ideas and surcharged with an electric affinity which arises from a full responsiveness to beauty and simplicity in art.

As she swings buoyantly on and upwards to the right, her optimism becomes accentuated by an intensity of affection for all living things.

Penetrating into the secrets of living, her mental eyes are as sharp as her pointed style, alert, keen to discover any new beauty lurking within. When she ventures forth on any tour of adventure, her fleet glance envisages each bit of quartz, each hidden water-melody, each sequestered nook, so that they one and all become tremulant with life, glowing elements of the creations she intends to weave. And weaving deftly, powerfully, she is able to produce a fictional tapestry as perfect as her connecting strokes, as delicately shaded as many of her written words. But since many of her final letters sweep away boldly, sympathetically she enters into the human and divine spirit of the people she creates, making them vital and true to themselves.

Her holograph, so well-balanced, so direct and positive, also indicates a decidedly practical turn. In a sense, she possesses a dual personality, comprehending the spiritual essence of things as well as the material. How lancelike are many of her upward strokes! Piercing the air joyously, her expressions and retorts are pointed, her language pungent.

There is never any doubt as to her sincere attitude toward friends and foes alike. She emphasizes her convictions as firmly and logically —many reasons being openly given—as she brings down many strokes of her pen. Personal and sensitive pride in excellent achievement animates her conscious mind—her signature. Intellectually a Madame Sans-Gêne when it comes to independence, there is no subject from flowers to cooking, from old men and maidens to young men and children, in which she does not take a real interest. Her pose redounds in a belief in healthful living—ever the means to her own development. A woman who lives as she writes, keenly human!

THE NEWCASTLE FORGOTTEN FANTASY LIBRARY

THE GLITTERING PLAIN by William Morris is the first title in The Newcastle Forgotten Fantasy Library, a new series of 26 adult fantasy classics. The works of William Morris (1834-1896) have influenced many writers of fantasy, such as Lord Dunsany, C.S. Lewis, and J.R.R. Tolkien, and continue to delight new generations of readers with their flights of high adventure in strange lands, their beautiful maidens and stalwart heroes. THE STORY OF THE GLITTERING PLAIN was the first of these romances. A must for the millions of Tolkien fans!

174 Pages   5½ x 8½ $2.45

THE SAGA OF ERIC BRIGHTEYES by H. Rider Haggard is a masterpiece of heroic fantasy by the creator of "SHE" and "KING SOLOMON'S MINES." No. 2 in the Newcastle Library of Forgotten Fantasy Classic Series. H. Rider Haggard achieved phenomenal popularity in his own day as a writer of fantastic romances and adventure tales, but today many of his lesser known works are all but forgotten. Such a novel is ERIC BRIGHTEYES, an heroic saga of bold adventure, treachery and dark sorcery. Haggard's biographer, Morton Cohen, said of ERIC BRIGHTEYES, "It is one of his best!" Illustrated.

304 Pages   5½ x 8½ $2.95

GHOSTS I HAVE MET Edited by John Kendrick Bangs. Here is a delightful collection of classic ghost stories by a master humorist. Here are spectres to make you smile instead of shiver, gleeful ghosts, amusing apparitions, and humorous haunts. Long out-of-print, this new edition of GHOSTS I HAVE MET, by the author of A HOUSE BOAT ON THE STYX, is an unabridged reproduction of the 1898 edition, with all the original illustrations by Peter Newell, A.B. Frost and Richards.

191 Pages   5½ x 8½ $2.45

NOW *from*

NEWCASTLE

These 4 Bestselling Books

YOU ARE WHAT YOU EAT
$2.25

EAT AND REDUCE
$2.45

VITAMIN COOKBOOK
$2.95

THE NATURAL WAY TO HEALTH
$2.95

by Victor Lindlahr

VIEWPOINT ON NUTRITION by Dr. Arnold Pike is a practical guide to proper nutrition and keeping fit. This fine book features interviews with Gaylord Hauser, Eddie Albert, Julie Harris, Sugar Ray Robinson, Dr. Linus Pauling, Marty Allen and many others. You will learn how to select exactly the right diet for you. Also contains the complete government report — Human Nutrition No. 2 by the U.S. Department of Agriculture. Introduction by Gaylord Hauser. Includes photographs of many celebrities who have appeared on Dr. Pike's nationally syndicated show. A Newcastle original! Dr. Arnold Pike has been called America's Mr. Media of Nutrition. He is the host of the coast to coast award-winning radio and TV Series 'Viewpoint on Nutrition.'
232 Pages   5½ x 8½ $2.95

Please check with your favorite Bookseller for any of the books listed on this page or order directly from:

NEWCASTLE PUBLISHING COMPANY, INC.
1521 North Vine St., Hollywood California 90028